Manna from Heaven

Down to Earth Kosher Recipes

ISBN 978-0-9792925-0-7

First Printing   May 2007   5,000 copies

WIMMER
COOKBOOKS

A CONSOLIDATED GRAPHICS COMPANY

800.548.2537   wimmerco.com

Food is an inextricable part of Judaism, both our religion and our culture. Our weekly observance of Shabbat and all of our holidays are marked by meals. Challah, chicken soup, the sweet and the bitter at Passover, hamantaschen, brachot: From the laws that regulate kosher food, what we may and may not eat, to the memories we treasure of our grandparents' kitchen, it is impossible to imagine or describe our faith without talking about food.

Thus, as Rudlin Torah Academy approached its 40th year, and we considered how to mark this anniversary, our thoughts naturally turned to food and cooking. Our staff and families pass recipes to each other, so why shouldn't we share them with the larger community?

When you look through these pages, you certainly will see the result of some very hard work. But you also may notice the astonishing variety of foods in the modern Jewish home, a rich texture drawn from thousands of years of ritual, tradition, and change.

Food changes as it reflects the journeys of a people. So many of us now live in suburbs, not the small villages or large cities of a few generations ago. Clearly, too, we do not eat all of the same foods as our ancestors in Eastern Europe or the Middle East or the Mediterranean. What would they have made of soy milk, or frozen latkes, or many of the kosher products we take for granted today? Yet there are familiar threads, ageless connections across time that bind us to our past and the future.

There has been much discussion in recent years of the pressures on Judaism, many reminders of the need for us to adjust to changing circumstances and yet hold on to what makes us uniquely Jewish. Surely we can find guidance in the way we maintain authentic Jewish cooking and come together, over the table, to celebrate life as a people.

When it came time to name this cookbook, our 40-year journey brought to mind another significant event in Jewish history, the liberation of the Hebrew people from bondage in Egypt and their 40 years of wandering in the desert before reaching the Promised Land. Their only sustenance during that time came from a miraculous food called *mon* (manna) which appeared each day, and which still carries the meaning of a wonderful, unexpected gift.

This is a memory we as a nation carry with us to this day, and it helps explain the mission of Rudlin Torah Academy, providing the children of our community with the daily gift of Torah, food for the soul.

We present this collection of recipes from our family in the hope that it will bring together your family and friends over the foods that have sustained our people.

Nannette Shor
Nannette Shor
Cookbook Committee Co-Chair

Judith Maizels
Cookbook Committee Co-Chair

Rabbi Hal Klestzick
Principal

About Our School

The Rudlin Torah Academy (RTA) in Richmond, Virginia was founded in 1966 as the Richmond Hebrew Day School. It began as the dream of a few parents who wanted to provide a Jewish education for their children. In its humble beginnings fewer than a dozen students began learning in a rented room at a local synagogue. By 1972 the school had grown so much that the community decided it was time to move the children into their own building. This would be the home for grades kindergarten through eighth grade for close to 30 years. In 1994 RTA also saw the need for a girls' high school and opened Shaarei Torah of Richmond (STOR), providing an excellent education not only for the girls in Richmond but for high school girls from all over the world. This school also had its beginnings in the rented rooms of a local synagogue and its out-of-town girls living with local families. STOR now has brand new educational facilities and a dormitory.

In 2002 RTA branched out even further, opening the first boys' yeshiva in Richmond, Yeshiva of Virginia (YVA), which serves the local families as well as boys from all over the country. Because of the enormous growth in our school population and program, the community saw the need for a new, state-of-the-art facility, so in 2001 ground was broken for a brand new school. In 2003 the elementary and middle school, along with STOR, moved to their new home in eastern Goochland County. YVA is located in the remodeled former K-8 school. Today more than 150 children are enrolled at the school's two campuses, serving boys and girls in grades K-12.

But no matter what the location, from small and humble to new and modern, RTA, STOR and YVA will always teach the mind and touch the heart by continuing to explore new technologies and methods in their quest to provide the very best Jewish and secular education available. The school's roots are deep in the Richmond community, but the fruits of its hard work and dedication have begun to spread across the country.

MANNA FROM HEAVEN
Down to Earth Recipes

Dear Reader,

Since the beginning of our history as a Jewish nation we have been a wandering people, making our homes all over the world. As we wandered through the desert for forty years G-d provided Manna which was described as being round, white and naturally tasted sweet and delicious, yet the Israelites had only to wish for it to have any other taste and miraculously it would. We have filled this cookbook with recipes designed to make kosher cooking easy, delicious and down to earth no matter where you live.

Scattered through these pages you also will find many historical, general, and Jewish food tidbits that we hope you will find interesting, informative and entertaining. We also hope that you enjoy the photos in our book as they are designed to allow you to use your imagination. Just as the Israelites wished for any taste when they ate manna, let the pictures inspire you to create your very own images and taste sensations.

When we started this project, we thought first about what we would like to see in a cookbook. Then we did our best to design one with you, the cook, in mind. Before you begin using this book, we would like to offer some simple guidelines to make this the most user friendly cookbook that you own.

All of the recipes have been triple tested to ensure that they are not only accurate but delicious. **Every page is color coded with green edges for pareve recipes, red edges for meat recipes and blue edges for dairy recipes.** In addition, each section of recipes is arranged from easiest to most ambitious. Along the way we'll let you know which recipes we think are extra special, and which ones our children loved. Our Effortless section is designed for that seasoned cook in a hurry who can throw a few things together and create a wonderful meal!

Our extended family at Rudlin Torah Academy is proud to present your family with the RTA cookbook. We hope you enjoy its unique blend of recipes as much as we enjoyed preparing it. And we hope it brings you and your family and friends together, only for joyous occasions, to celebrate the miracle of Jewish life today.

Enjoy and eat well,
Your friends at the
Rudlin Torah Academy
Richmond, Virginia

COOKBOOK COMMITTEE

Co-Chairs

Judith Maizels

Nannette Shor

Proofreaders

Rene Gold

Kate Moore

Rachel Sattler

Nancy R. Weiss

Fundraising

Nathan and
Nannette Shor

Writers

Rabbi Yosef Bart

Noa Klestzick

Judith Maizels

Tony Wharton

Recipe Computer Entry

Yonatan Cantor

Rene Gold

Anita Kozakewicz

Melissa Krumbein

Ella Schwartz

Director of Marketing & Development

Beth Bendheim

Chapter Editors

EFFORTLESS
Noa Klestzick

Judith Maizels

BREADS
Rivka Bart

APPETIZERS, DIPS AND SPREADS
Tony and Karen Wharton

SOUPS
Gail Moskowitz

SALADS
Mary Lee Cantor

ENTRÉES
Shirley Brown

Michelle Maistelman

SIDE DISHES AND VEGETABLES
Rivka Bart

Nannette Shor

DESSERTS
Shifra Freedlander

Susana Kenigsberg

OUR SPONSORS

Bronze Level

The Colby Family

The Shor Family

Contributors

Morty & Shirley Brown

Andy & Melissa Brownstein

Ted Sandler, Abbie Fields & Noah Sandler

Deborah Sterling

The C. F. Sauer Company

Supporters

C&F Bank

Mr. & Mrs. Stuart Cantor

Designer Deliveries

Shifra Freedlander

Rick & Linda Gary

Edythe Hoffman

Wendy & Randy Howard & Family

Mr. & Mrs. Jay Ipson

Mr. & Mrs. Malcolm Kalman

Miss Yali Bajtner & Mr. Ariel Klestzick

Special Thank You's

Computer Resolutions
for Web site design and technical assistance

Designer Deliveries
for storing the Manna from Heaven cookbooks

Special thanks to Kenneth Bendheim, Susie Cantor, Michelle Cantor, Susan Gaible, Lin Hardy, Orly Lewis, Terry Lynn, Harriet Rochkind and Anna Yolkut for their time and expertise. We are truly grateful to the additional friends and families who made generous financial gifts towards the publishing of this cookbook.

RECIPE CONTRIBUTORS AND TESTERS

To our recipe contributors and testers, we extend our deepest appreciation for the immeasurable donations of your time, your kitchens, your families, and most of all, your taste buds. This cookbook would not exist without your help. Due to space consideration, we were unable to use all of the recipes submitted. We sincerely hope we have not overlooked anyone.

Sam Abrash	Victoria Caplan	Ilana Gimpelevich
Paula Altman	Sari Chait	Ray Glass
Deborah Arenstein	Teiby Chait	Limor Glazer-Schwam
Dora J. Baron	Audrey Chumbris	Amy Goel
Rivka Bart	Sandee Coen	Rene and Mike Gold
Helen Bellah	Aldebaran Cohen	Diane Goldberg
Hilary Bender	Dalia Cohen	Rachel Goldberg
Jennifer Bendheim	Debbie Colby	Joan Goodstein
Kenneth R. Bendheim	Carmel Colon	Leah Greenman
Dee Berkowitz	Cheryl Conradt-Eberlin	Helen Griffin
Dell Berlinerman	Ruth Corcia	Jana Gross
Marcia Bernstein	Natalie Dardick	Jacob A. Haine
Danya Binshtok	Heather Dinkin	Rebecca Haine
Esther Binshtok	Rivy Dolin	Judy and Arthur Harrow
Shannon Blackwell	Jeannie Dortch	Dawn Hersh
Francine Blum	Sarah Drucker	Nancy Hersh
Beth Bradford	Deane R. Dubansky	Regina Herzog
Gladys Brenner	Barbara Egel	Helen and Hal Horwitz
Shirley Brown	S. Eiferman	Sheila Hyman
Aliza Bulow	Chanie Farber	Laurie Janus
Deborah and Paul Cantor	Judy Feldstein	David Kalman
Eric Cantor	Nechama Finer	Rebecca Kalman-Winston
Joan Cantor	Sharyl Freedlander	Willa Kalman
Mary Lee Cantor	Shifra Freedlander	Pat Kelley
Michelle Cantor	Nathalie and Scott Gaeser	Kolman Kenigsberg
Shirley Cantor	Aviva Gershman	Rositta Kenigsberg
Susie Cantor	Bill Gibbs	Susana Kenigsberg

Evelyn Kessler

Noa Klestzick

Robin Kocen

Sylvia Kootner

Shainie Kovitz

Anita Kozakewicz

Nechomi Kranz

Cynthia Krumbein

Melissa and Jason
Krumbein

Todd LaMaskin

Harriet Lapkin

Hedy Lapkin

Amy Beth Lehman

Judy Lessin

Muriel Levin

Rochelle Levin

Leora Lewis

Orly Lewis

Edythe Lichtenstein

Marilyn Liroff

Marilyn Lowenstein

Terry Lynn

Miriam S. Lyss

Michelle Maistelman

Judith and Max Maizels

Bonita Makdad

Harriett Malkin

Pearl Karp Markham

Patty Colby Meeks

Shari Menlowe-Barck

Chaya Meyer

Mindy Michaels

Michelle Miller

Kate Moore

Andi Moskowitz

Gail Moskowitz

Debbie Mullian

Julie Mullian

Sylvia Newman

Nattie Ohlinger

Ilene Paley

Leah Paley

Mimi Parizer

Lorraine Pearson

Debbie Plotnick

Kay Politis, obm

Debbie Rauch

Audrey Reich

Harriet Rochkind

Fran Rojas

Sharon Ron

Karen Roodman

Toby Rosenthal

Bonnie Roskind

Jay Rue

Ronit Saar

Jane Samora

Rachel Sattler

Susan Schaefer

Terry Schultz

Ella and Dave Schwartz

Linda Shait

Ellen Shapiro

Connie Sharp

Robin Shell

Pam Shipley

Nannette and Nathan Shor

Leah Shull

Lynn Simonoff

Amy Singer

Michael Ann Singer

Joy Sisisky

Susan Sisisky

Leah Skaist

Anne Woods Sonenklar

Micki Spector

Marcy Stein

Linda Thomas

Laurie Topaz

Marissa Weill

Margaret Weinberg

Todd Weinberg

Rachel Weinberg-Rue

Dan and Beth Weintraub

Nancy R. Weiss

Randi Weiss

Karen and Tony Wharton

Rocky White

Connie Williams

Lindsay Wood

Joyce Zasler

Dana Zedd

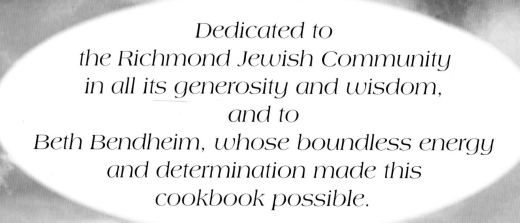

Dedicated to
the Richmond Jewish Community
in all its generosity and wisdom,
and to
Beth Bendheim, whose boundless energy
and determination made this
cookbook possible.

Table of Contents

Effortless

This Effortless section is designed for the seasoned cook in a hurry who can throw a few things together and create a wonderful meal! Enjoy.

*The manna was an effortless
and miraculous daily provision of food
which was of great nutritive value.*

(Rav S.R. Hirsch, Parshas Chukas)

BEFORE YOU BEGIN...

KITCHEN MUST HAVE
Immersion blender

PANTRY STAPLES
Cajun seasoning
Seasoned salt
Vegetable spray
Pareve soup mix: onion, chicken, mushroom and beef

GREAT SHORTCUTS
Shredded potatoes
Garlic in a jar
Frozen puff pastry

APPETIZERS

Deli Roll – Roll out 2 puff pastry sheets, spread with your favorite mustard and a single layer of your favorite deli meat, roll up jelly-roll style. Brush lightly with beaten egg for shine, bake at 375° until brown, 25-35 minutes. Slice and serve!

Wild Wings – For every pound of chicken wings (cut in half, tips discarded) or drumettes, mix together: 1 tablespoon soy sauce, 2 crushed garlic cloves, ½ teaspoon garlic powder and ½ cup brown sugar. Pour over wings and bake 45 minutes covered and 30 minutes uncovered at 350°.

Hot and Spicy Wings – Use chicken wings (cut in half, tips discarded) or drumettes. Sprinkle with garlic powder and paprika. Mix with a small amount of oil, bake covered at 350° for 45 minutes. Add hot and spicy duck sauce and bake uncovered 30 minutes more.

Quick Knishes – Use either leftover meat, chicken or mashed potatoes. Add fried onions and an egg and wrap in puff pastry squares. Brush with egg wash and bake at 350° until brown, 30-45 minutes.

Sweet and Sour Salami – Mix a 12-ounce bottle chili sauce, ½ cup brown sugar, and 1 tablespoon mustard in an ovenproof baking dish. Add 2 pounds bullet salami, thickly sliced, toss to coat, and bake 30 minutes uncovered at 350°. Serve hot.

ENTRÉES

Chicken Kishke Pastry – Defrost kishke until easy to slice. Roll out puff pastry sheet and cut into 9 squares. Place 1 kishke round and 1 small piece chicken cutlet in center of each square. Wrap pastry dough completely around filling, place seam side down on greased cookie sheet. Brush with egg wash and bake 45 minutes to 1 hour at 350° or until brown.

Effortless

Pastrami Chicken – Using chicken cutlet thinly sliced, dip into Italian dressing, then coat with seasoned bread crumbs. Place a slice of pastrami on the cutlet, roll, and place on greased cookie sheet with the seam side down. Pour a small amount of apple juice on cookie sheet and spray chicken liberally with cooking spray. Bake 45 minutes to 1 hour at 350°.

Pepper Steak – Brown 2 pounds of pepper steak in a large skillet. Add ½ cup French dressing, 3 tablespoons soy sauce and 1 cup water. Simmer 30 minutes. While it cooks, slice up 2 green peppers, 2 onions and 2 stalks celery. Add to pot, cover and simmer another 45 minutes or until tender. Serve over rice.

Terrific Turkey – Soften ½ stick margarine. Mix in 1½ tablespoons each of sage, rosemary and thyme (preferably freshly chopped) and rub on turkey (you can also rub it under the skin). Pour 2 cups chicken stock (powdered is best) into pan around bottom of turkey, and bake covered according to directions for turkey size. Baste occasionally.

Best Brisket – Use either a foil bag or 2 sheets heavy duty foil, cut about 5 inches larger than brisket. Use a brisket with some fat. Spread ketchup on 1 sheet of foil, sprinkle with onion flakes, place brisket on the ketchup and spread ketchup and onion flakes on the meat. Crimp sheets together to make a bag and place it on a cookie sheet. Bake 1½ hours at 350°, flip the bag and continue baking until meat is done. Use juices as a sauce.

Oven Fried Cajun Chicken – Dip chicken pieces in lightly beaten egg, then dredge in a mixture of flour, a small amount of matzo meal, and generous amounts of salt, pepper, paprika, onion powder, garlic powder and Cajun spice. Place on sprayed and oiled cookie sheet. Drizzle oil on pieces of chicken and spray with cooking spray. Bake at 350° for 1 hour or until crisp.

Chicken Pot Pie for the Family – Use 2 frozen pie crusts and 2 sheets puff pastry. Melt 1 stick margarine in a pan, add 6 tablespoons flour, and gradually pour in boiling chicken stock. Stir until thick and smooth. Add pieces of leftover chicken and 1 bag of your favorite frozen vegetables. Salt and pepper to taste and add 1 egg. Pour into pie crusts, roll out puff pastry, place on top and shape to fit. Brush with egg and bake at 350° for 45 minutes or until puffy and brown.

FISH DISHES

The Best Tuna Salad – Mix white (albacore) tuna with a dash of lemon juice, salt, pepper and mayonnaise. Add either thyme or dill to taste.

Oven Fried Gefilte Fish – Slightly defrost gefilte fish loaf, cut into ½-inch slices, and coat with seasoned bread crumbs. Bake 30 minutes at 375° in a well-oiled pan, turn and bake 15 minutes more.

Quick Fix Fish Dish #1 – Using any type fish filet, such as flounder, tilapia, or salmon, sprinkle with oregano, salt, pepper, onion or garlic powder or any of your favorite seasonings. Pat with butter and sprinkle with lemon juice. Either bake, broil, grill or poach in foil until fish is done and flakes easily.

Quick Fix Fish Dish #2 – Use either tilapia or salmon fillets. Dredge in seasoned bread crumbs, place in a well-oiled pan, and pour any brand of French dressing liberally over fish. Bake 20-30 minutes at 350° until edges crisp.

SIDE DISHES AND SALADS

Butternut Squash Soufflé – slice a medium-size butternut squash lengthwise and remove seeds. Place face down in pan and bake 45 minutes at 375°. Scoop out flesh and mash. Add ¾ cup each of flour, sugar, and oil; add 4 eggs and mix. Bake in greased casserole at 375° for another 45 minutes.

Potato Kugel – Using a food processor, shred 5 medium-large peeled potatoes and place in a large bowl. Then purée 5 medium-large peeled potatoes and a large onion, add 5 eggs, ¼ cup oil, a lot of salt and pepper, and mix everything into the shredded potatoes. Preheat ¼-inch oil in a 9 x 13 x 2-inch pan and add the mixture. Bake 1½-2 hours at 350° until brown and firm.

Easy "Not" Ratatouille – Sauté a lot of onions and garlic in olive oil. Add unpeeled, chunked fresh zucchini, and sauté a few more minutes. Add large jar of your favorite pasta sauce and ¼-½ cup sugar. Add salt and pepper and Italian spices to taste. Cook on low heat or in the oven at 350° for 1 hour or until soft.

Stewed Veggies – Coat a large lidded skillet with ¼-inch oil, and add a layer of sliced onion rings. In ⅓ of the skillet place white potatoes, peeled and cut into large chunks; in the next ⅓ place sweet potatoes or yams, peeled and cut into large chunks; in the last ⅓ place frozen vegetables — peas, green beans, cauliflower or any other favorite. Top with another layer of sliced onion rings, sprinkle with oil and season liberally with salt and pepper. Cover skillet and cook 1½-2 hours on medium-low heat. Do not touch until ready to serve.

Broccoli Kugel – Mix together 2 (16-ounce) packages thawed chopped broccoli or broccoli cuts, 5 eggs, 4 tablespoons mayonnaise, and 1 package onion soup mix. Pour into a greased 9 x 13 x 2-inch pan. Sprinkle with cornflake crumbs and paprika and bake 30-40 minutes at 350°.

Broccoli Quiche – Mix together 20 ounces thawed chopped broccoli, 6 eggs, 6 tablespoons flour, 1 pound cottage cheese and 1 package shredded Cheddar cheese. Bake in a 9 x 13 x 2-inch pan at 350° for 30-40 minutes or until firm and slightly browned.

Baked Ziti – Prepare 1 pound ziti according to package directions, mix in 1½ jars of your favorite pasta sauce, 1 package shredded Cheddar cheese and ⅛ cup vegetable oil. Top with more shredded Cheddar. Bake at 350° covered for 30 minutes and then uncovered for 15 minutes more.

Rice and Cheese – Using a short grain white rice, cook rice according to package directions. About 5 minutes before rice is done, add shredded Cheddar cheese and mix together. Let cook 5 minutes. Broccoli can be added for additional flavor.

Easy Tuna Noodle Casserole – Cook 1 package macaroni and mix with 2 cans tuna, ¾ cup mayonnaise and 6 ounces shredded Cheddar cheese. Sprinkle more Cheddar cheese on top and bake uncovered at 350° until golden brown.

Broccoli Salad – Mix 4 cups fresh broccoli florets, chopped red onion, and golden raisins. Add salted cashew halves before serving. Dressing: In a jar, mix ¾ cup sugar, ½ cup vinegar, 1 cup mayonnaise and ⅓ cup water. Add to salad when ready to serve.

Delicious Cole Slaw – Shred green peppers, 2 pounds carrots, 3 green onions and 1 cabbage. Mix dressing of ¾ cup sugar, ½ cup vinegar, 1 cup mayonnaise and ⅓ cup water.

Caesar Salad – Chop romaine lettuce and add croutons and Parmesan cheese. For the dressing, mix 4 chopped garlic cloves, ¼ cup water, ¼ cup vinegar, ¼ cup sugar, 1 cup mayonnaise, 1 squeeze mustard and 1 tablespoon dried basil. Add to salad when ready to serve.

Leafy Salad – Combine romaine lettuce, sliced kiwi, strawberries, mango and cucumber. For the dressing, mix equal parts Italian dressing and honey.

Bagel Chip Salad – Combine romaine lettuce, cherry tomatoes, red onion, ¼ cup craisins, and crushed bagel chips. Make dressing from ½ cup mayonnaise ½ cup sugar, ½ cup vinegar and garlic powder.

Zucchini Vegetable Barley Soup – Sauté 1 onion, and any of your favorite vegetables sliced or chopped (zucchini, carrots, celery, potatoes, sweet potatoes, rutabaga, broccoli). Fill pot with water, bring to a boil and add 4 tablespoons pareve chicken soup powder and ½-1 cup barley. Add salt and pepper to taste and cook 1 hour. Add 1 bag frozen vegetables and cook 1 more hour. The longer it cooks the better it tastes.

DESSERTS

Fancy Pears – Purée thawed frozen strawberries in syrup. Add canned pear halves and refrigerate several hours.

Strawberry Applesauce – Place frozen strawberries in a bowl and thaw. Add a jar of applesauce and whip together with immersion blender.

Apple Cobbler – Spray pie pan and add 1 can apple or peach filling. Top with a mixture of 1 stick of margarine (room temperature), 1 cup sugar, ¾ cup flour, ½ teaspoon cinnamon. Bake at 350° until golden brown.

Ambrosia – Whip non-dairy whipped topping, add canned Mandarin oranges, crushed pineapple and thawed berries (strawberries, raspberries, or blueberries). Whip once more and refrigerate until ready to serve.

Easy-as-Pie Pies – Whip 8 ounces non-dairy topping. Fold in 1 can lemon pie filling and pour into a graham cracker crust. Chill until ready to serve. For chocolate flavor, use 1 package of instant chocolate pudding, 1 cup soy milk and 8 ounces whipped topping. Garnish if desired. Refrigerate until ready to serve.

Breads

"...Moshe said to them,
'this is the bread that Hashem
has given you to eat.' "

(Parshas B'shalach, 16, 15)

*The Manna anecdotes
in this section are culled from
the words of our sages in
the commentaries and
Midrash.

Just a Reminder...
green = pareve   red = meat   blue = dairy

When the
Jews saw the phenomenon of
manna for the first time, they exclaimed
"Man hu," meaning "what is it?" Hence the
Hebrew word, "man" for manna.

No Need to Knead Challah

Yields: 8 loaves

6 packets quick rise yeast
2½ cups plus 2 tablespoons sugar
4 cups warm water
5 pounds plus 3 cups bread flour
2 tablespoons salt

8 extra large eggs
1½ cups oil
1 egg plus 3 tablespoons water for
    wash
Sesame or poppy seeds, optional

Dissolve yeast plus 2 tablespoons sugar in 2 cups warm water in a medium bowl. Set aside. In an extra large bowl, mix flour and salt together and make a well in the center. In a separate bowl mix together remaining sugar, eggs and oil.

Add yeast mixture and 2 additional cups of warm water to sugar, egg and oil mixture. Slowly pour egg and yeast mixture into the well in the flour and mix. Make sure that all the flour is mixed into the dough. Mix only enough to combine all the ingredients. Cover with a damp cloth and either leave in the refrigerator overnight or let rise at room temperature until doubled in bulk, 2-3 hours. In the morning, remove from refrigerator and place on a clean surface. Divide up dough into 8 portions, roll each portion into 3 ropes and braid loaves.

Spray baking sheets or large loaf pans and place challah on or in them. Cover again with damp cloth and allow to rise about 2 hours. Preheat oven to 350°. Beat egg with water and brush on challah. Sprinkle with either sesame or poppy seeds if desired. Bake 25-30 minutes until loaves are golden brown. Remove from oven and place on racks until cool. Challah may be wrapped in foil and frozen.

Prepare Ahead of Time

The righteous found the manna at their doorsteps, the average needed only to go out of their homes, and the evil had to wander a distance to gather the manna.

PUMPKIN BREAD

Yields: 36 medium muffins or 3, 8 x 8-inch pans

3½ cups flour
3 cups sugar
1 tablespoon cinnamon
2 teaspoons baking soda

1 cup oil
1 (15-ounce) can pumpkin
4 eggs
⅔ cup water

Preheat oven to 350°. Mix all ingredients together. Pour into 3 greased 8 x 8-inch pans or 36 medium muffin tins. Bake 30-45 minutes.

ZUCCHINI BREAD

Yields: 20 servings

2 cups sugar
1 cup oil
3 eggs
3 cups all-purpose flour
½ teaspoon baking powder
1 teaspoon baking soda

1 teaspoon salt
1 teaspoon cinnamon
1 cup chopped nuts
2 cups shredded zucchini
2 teaspoons vanilla

Preheat oven to 350°. Mix ingredients in order listed above. Pour into 2 greased loaf pans. Bake 45 minutes or until toothpick comes out clean.

STRAWBERRY BREAD ·

Yields: 6-8 servings

1½ cups flour
½ teaspoon baking soda
½ teaspoon salt
1 cup sugar
½ cup chopped pecans

1 teaspoon orange or vanilla extract
1¼ cups strawberries, chopped
2 eggs, beaten
⅔ cup oil

Preheat oven to 350°. Mix flour, baking soda, salt, sugar and pecans. Mix extract, strawberries, eggs and oil in mixer. Add dry ingredients and mix until combined. Bake 1 hour in a greased 9 x 5-inch loaf pan.

The manna's taste transformed into the taste of whatever an individual wished it to be, whether the foods required cooking or baking or were normally eaten raw.

CREATE YOUR OWN MUFFINS

Yields: 12-24 muffins

1 egg
½ cup milk
¼ cup vegetable oil
1½ cups all-purpose flour
¼ cup brown sugar

¼ cup sugar
2 teaspoons baking powder
½ teaspoon salt
¾ cup of blueberries

Preheat oven to 375°. Blend egg, milk and oil. Combine flour, sugars, baking powder and salt, and add to liquid mixture. Stir until just smooth. Fold in blueberries. Fill greased or lined muffin cups ⅔ full. Bake 20-25 minutes.

Substitute other fruit, raisins or chocolate chips for the blueberries to make muffins your own.

BANANA LOAF BREAD

Yields: 8-10 servings

2 eggs
½ cup oil
1 cup sugar
1 teaspoon vanilla
1 teaspoon baking powder
1 teaspoon baking soda

4 tablespoons milk
2 large or 3 small over-ripened
    bananas, mashed
2 cups flour
1 cup chocolate chips

Preheat oven to 350°. Mix eggs, oil, sugar, vanilla, baking powder, baking soda, milk and mashed bananas. Add flour and mix. Add chocolate chips. Pour into a greased loaf pan and bake 60-70 minutes.

The manna was
absorbed entirely into the
limbs without creating any
waste materials.

PROCESSOR POPOVERS

Yields: 10-12 popovers

2 large eggs
1 cup milk

½ teaspoon salt
1 cup sifted all-purpose flour

Place eggs, milk and salt in a processor with metal chopping blade, and pulse 3 seconds nonstop. Add flour, sprinkling it over surface of beaten egg mixture. Pulse 10 seconds nonstop. Scrape down sides and pulse 5 seconds. Let batter stand 30 minutes before baking. Preheat oven to 450°. Grease a standard muffin pan well. Five minutes before you're ready to bake popovers, set pan in oven to preheat. Remove pan from oven, ladle batter into each muffin cup, filling ⅔ full, no more. Return pan to oven and bake, uncovered, 25-30 minutes, or until nicely puffed and brown. Serve.

POPOVERS

Yields: 12 large popovers

4 cups milk
8 eggs
4 cups flour

1½ heaping tablespoons salt
2¼ cups grated Swiss cheese

Place a popover pan in oven. Heat oven and pan to 350°. Gently warm milk over low heat and set aside. Whisk eggs until frothy and slowly whisk in milk (so as not to cook the eggs). Set mixture aside. Sift flour with salt. Slowly add this dry mixture to milk and eggs and gently combine until mostly smooth. Remove popover pan from oven and spray with non-stick vegetable spray. While batter is still slightly warm or room temperature (definitely not cool), fill each popover cup ¾ full. Top each popover with approximately 2½ tablespoons grated Swiss cheese. Bake 50 minutes, rotating pan half a turn after 15 minutes of baking. Remove from oven, remove from pan and serve immediately.

PEACH BREAD

Yields: 2 loaves

½ cup unsalted margarine
1 cup sugar
3 eggs
2¾ cups flour
1½ teaspoons baking powder
1 teaspoon salt
½ teaspoon baking soda

1½ teaspoons cinnamon
2 cups fresh or frozen peaches, diced
3 tablespoons frozen orange
    concentrate, thawed
1 teaspoon vanilla
Raw sugar to taste

Preheat oven to 350°. Grease and flour two 9-inch loaf pans. Cream margarine and gradually add sugar. Add eggs, one at a time, beating well after each addition. Sift flour, baking powder, salt, baking soda and cinnamon together. Add dry ingredients in batches, alternating with peaches. Stir in orange juice concentrate and vanilla. Spoon into 2 loaf pans. Sprinkle with raw sugar. Bake 1 hour. Cool in pan 10 minutes, remove and cool completely before slicing.

Note about peaches: If using fresh peaches, peel first by dropping into boiling water for a few seconds. If using frozen peaches, use 1 (16-ounce) package and partially defrost first.

Chopped pecans would add great flavor if added to batter before baking.

MONKEY BREAD

Yields: 10-12 servings

½ cup sugar
2 tablespoons cinnamon
1 cup brown sugar
1 stick butter

2 tablespoons water
2 (16-ounce) cans crescent, biscuit or
    pastry dough
1 cup chopped pecans, optional

Preheat oven to 350°. In a small bowl, mix sugar and cinnamon. Set aside. Grease a Bundt pan and coat bottom of pan with half of sugar mixture. In a small saucepan, melt together brown sugar, butter and water until well blended. Take one can of dough, break off pieces, and roll into 1-inch balls. Roll each ball in cinnamon sugar and place in Bundt pan. Spoon half the brown sugar-butter mixture over dough. Repeat process with remaining dough. Add nuts to top, if desired. Bake 35-40 minutes.

As a variation, you can melt 2 tablespoons of butter in Bundt pan. Roll dough in cinnamon sugar and layer without the brown sugar. It makes a lighter dessert that is not as sweet.

Biscuit dough is the traditional way to make this bread.

BLUEBERRY-LEMON BREAD

Yields: 8-10 slices

1½ cups all-purpose flour
1 teaspoon baking powder
¼ teaspoon salt
6 tablespoons unsalted butter,
    room temperature
1⅓ cups sugar

2 large eggs
2 teaspoons lemon zest
½ cup milk
1½ cups fresh blueberries
    (if frozen, thaw and drain)
3 tablespoons fresh lemon juice

Preheat oven to 325°. Grease an 8-inch or 9-inch loaf pan. Mix flour, baking powder and salt in a small bowl. In a large bowl using an electric mixer, cream butter with 1 cup sugar until mixture is fluffy. Add eggs one at a time, beating well. Add lemon zest. Begin to mix in dry ingredients in small portions, alternating with milk, and ending with dry ingredients. Mix in blueberries by hand. Pour batter into loaf pan. Bake 1 hour 15 minutes or until golden and toothpick inserted in center comes out clean.

Just before loaf finishes baking, bring remaining sugar and lemon juice to a boil in a small saucepan, stirring until the sugar dissolves.

After removing bread from oven, leave in pan but set pan on sheet of wax paper or foil. Pierce top of loaf several times with a toothpick. Pour hot lemon mixture over top (some likely will run over the sides) and allow to soak in. Cool 30 minutes in pan, then turn out onto rack and cool completely.

GOAT CHEESE FOCACCIA

Yields: 8 servings

1 loaf frozen white bread dough or
   frozen challah dough
1½ teaspoons olive oil

1 medium yellow onion, sliced
4 ounces goat cheese, crumbled
Salt and pepper, to taste

Preheat oven to 425°. Thaw bread dough completely. Pour ¼ teaspoon olive oil into hands and oil dough all over. Press dough into lightly oiled 9-inch cast iron skillet.

Sauté onions in 1 teaspoon olive oil until soft and caramelized. Scatter top of dough with onions and goat cheese. Sprinkle with salt and freshly ground pepper. Drizzle very lightly with olive oil. Bake 20 minutes or until browned. Serve immediately.

Whereas our
food rises from the earth, and
dew descends from the sky, the manna
descended from the sky and the dew
covering it rose from the earth.

Morning Glory Muffins

Yields: 18 muffins

2 cups all-purpose flour
1¼ cups white sugar
2 teaspoons baking soda
2 teaspoons ground cinnamon
½ teaspoon salt
1½ cups carrots, grated
1½ cups apple, peeled and grated

¾ cup flaked coconut
½ cup dates, pitted and chopped
½ cup pecans, chopped
3 eggs, beaten
½ cup vegetable oil
½ teaspoon vanilla extract

Preheat oven to 375°. Lightly oil 18 muffin cups, or coat with nonstick cooking spray. In a large mixing bowl, combine flour, sugar, baking soda, cinnamon and salt. In a second bowl, combine carrots, apples, coconut, dates and pecans. Stir in eggs, oil and vanilla. Add this mixture to the dry ingredients; stir until smooth. Spoon or scoop batter into prepared muffin pans. Bake 18-20 minutes or until a toothpick inserted into the center of a muffin comes out clean.

SOUTHWESTERN CORNBREAD

Yields: 10-12 servings

1 (8-ounce) box cornbread mix
1 teaspoon sugar
1 teaspoon baking powder
1½ cups grated Cheddar cheese
1 onion, chopped
1 (11-ounce) can yellow corn, drained

3 jalapeño peppers or
    1 (4-ounce) can diced green chilis
3 eggs, beaten
2 cups milk
½ cup vegetable oil

Preheat oven to 400°. Mix together cornbread mix, sugar and baking powder. Add cheese, onion, corn and peppers, mix well. Add beaten eggs, milk, and oil.

Pour into a greased 9 x 13-inch dish (batter will be thin, almost soupy). Bake 35-40 minutes.

For a dryer version, cut into pieces, reduce oven temperature to 200° and bake a little longer. Refrigerate leftovers.

Canned chipotle chilis also can be substituted for the peppers.

The manna would last only one day (except for Friday's portion), after which it would miraculously turn wormy and moldy, with an offensive odor.

BUTTERMILK BISCUITS

Yields: 10 servings

¼ cup shortening
2 cups flour
1 tablespoon sugar
2 teaspoons baking powder

1 teaspoon salt
½ teaspoon baking soda
¾ cup plus 2 tablespoons buttermilk

Preheat oven to 450°. Cut shortening into flour, sugar, baking powder, salt and baking soda with a pastry blender until fine crumbs form. Stir in just enough buttermilk so dough leaves sides of bowl and forms a round. Do not overmix.

Place dough on a slightly floured surface and knead about 30 seconds. Roll to ½-inch thickness. Cut with a floured 2½-inch biscuit cutter. Place on an ungreased cookie sheet. (For crusty sides, place 1-inch apart, or let touch for softer sides.) Bake 10-12 minutes or until golden brown. Remove immediately from cookie sheet.

SWEET POTATO BISCUITS

Yields: 12 biscuits

2 medium sweet potatoes
   (about 1 pound)
2¼ cups buttermilk baking mix
½ cup golden brown sugar, firmly
   packed

1 teaspoon cinnamon
⅛ teaspoon nutmeg, freshly ground
¼ teaspoon ground cloves
3 tablespoons water

Preheat oven to 350°. Grease a large baking sheet. Pierce sweet potatoes and cook in microwave, 5-8 minutes or until very tender. Let cool. Peel, transfer to a large mixing bowl, and mash thoroughly. Stir in buttermilk baking mix, brown sugar, cinnamon, nutmeg and cloves. Add water, one tablespoon at a time, until a soft dough forms.

Turn out dough onto a lightly floured surface. Roll out into ½-inch thick round. Cut out biscuits with a 3-inch biscuit or cookie cutter. Gather scraps into ball, roll out dough, and repeat until dough is used up. Place on baking sheet and bake until golden brown, about 18 minutes. Biscuits will only rise slightly. Transfer to a cooling rack. Serve warm.

You can also serve these with cinnamon butter: Beat together 1 stick softened butter, ¼ cup confectioners' sugar, 1 teaspoon vanilla extract and 1 teaspoon ground cinnamon until well blended and fluffy.

ZESTY LEMON SCONES

Yields: 12 servings

2 cups all-purpose flour
½ cup sugar
1 tablespoon baking powder
½ teaspoon salt

2 tablespoons lemon zest
1¼ cups heavy cream
3 tablespoons unsalted butter, melted

Preheat oven to 425°. Combine flour, ¼ cup sugar, baking powder and salt in a mixing bowl, then stir in 1 tablespoon of lemon zest. Add cream and stir until it just comes together in a dough. Empty dough onto a lightly floured surface. Knead gently until the dough holds together, then shape into a 10-inch round, about ½-inch high. Cut into 12 wedges.

Grease a large baking sheet and transfer the dough triangles to the sheet. In a small bowl, combine remaining ¼ cup sugar with remaining tablespoon lemon zest to make lemon sugar. Brush scones with melted butter, then sprinkle lemon sugar on top. Bake until light golden brown, about 15 minutes. Transfer to a cooling rack. Serve warm.

These are best when fresh from the oven. After they cool, they can be kept for perhaps a day in sealed plastic bags and then briefly microwaved.

LIGHT-AS-A-CLOUD CHEDDAR BISCUITS

Yields: 10 servings

1½ cups all-purpose flour
½ cup yellow cornmeal
2 tablespoons sugar
1½ teaspoons baking powder
¾ teaspoon kosher salt
½ teaspoon baking soda
½ cup unsalted butter, cold, cut into
    ½-inch cubes

1½ cups sharp Cheddar cheese, grated
2 large eggs
¾ cup buttermilk
1 tablespoon finely chopped canned
    chipotle chilies
½ cup chopped fresh parsley
1 tablespoon heavy cream

Preheat oven to 425°. Combine flour, cornmeal, sugar, baking powder, salt and baking soda in a food processor. Add butter, cutting it in with quick pulses of the processor until mixture resembles coarse crumbs. Add cheese, cut in with quick pulses. Transfer flour mixture to a large bowl.

Whisk 1 egg in a small bowl, add buttermilk and stir. Add chipotles and parsley. Make a well in center of flour mixture; pour buttermilk mixture into well. Mix just until evenly moistened and dough barely holds together. Do not overmix.

Turn dough onto a well-floured surface. Knead briefly, about 10 times. Pat out into ¾-inch thick round. With biscuit cutter (preferably 3-inch), cut out biscuits and transfer to an ungreased baking sheet, about an inch apart. Gather up dough scraps, combine just enough to hold together, and form new ¾-inch thick round. Cut out biscuits and repeat until dough is used up.

Beat remaining egg with cream, brush onto biscuits. Bake 18 minutes or until golden and toothpick comes out clean. Transfer to a rack, cool slightly. Serve warm.

PIZZA DOUGH

Yields: 2 pies

1 package dry yeast
1 teaspoon sugar
1 cup warm water

½ teaspoon salt
2 tablespoons canola or olive oil
2½ cups flour

Preheat oven to 425°. Dissolve yeast and sugar in water. Let sit 5 minutes. Add salt, oil and flour and knead until smooth. Cover and let rise until doubled in size.

Recipe can easily be doubled.

Bread sticks variation: *Preheat oven to 400°. Dough can also be cut into 24 balls and rolled out into sticks. Just roll in your favorite spices, toppings (cheese, oregano, salt, garlic, etc.) and bake 10-15 minutes until golden brown. Serve warm.*

No matter how much or how little a person collected of the manna, when he brought it home, it miraculously became the same "Omer Lagulgolet" – an "omer" (standard measure) per person.

DINNER ROLLS

Yields: 12 dinner rolls

1 package dry yeast
1 cup warm water
1 teaspoon salt

1 egg
2 tablespoons shortening
2¼ cups flour

Dissolve yeast in water and allow to sit 5 minutes. Mix in salt, egg, shortening and 1 cup flour. Add remaining flour and continue to stir, then knead until smooth. Let rise in a covered bowl until doubled in size. Cut dough into 12 pieces and shape into rolls. Place on a greased cookie sheet and bake at 350° about 15 minutes or until golden brown. Serve warm.

Variation: Balls of dough can also be placed in a muffin tin.

On Fridays, the Jews collected a
"double" portion. Actually, they gathered the same
amount as they did daily, but upon arriving at home, the
manna miraculously "doubled in bulk," providing
Shabbat food as well.

MOROCCAN OLIVE BREAD

Yields: 1 Medium Loaf

1½ teaspoons active dry yeast
1 cup warm water
2½ cups all-purpose flour, plus more
    for kneading

½ teaspoon salt
½ teaspoon anise seeds
6 pitted green or black olives, sliced
    crosswise

In a small bowl, mix yeast with ¼ cup of water. Let stand 5 minutes. Sift 2½ cups flour into a medium bowl. Stir in salt and anise. With a wooden spoon, stir in yeast and remaining ¾ cup of water until a sticky dough forms. Transfer dough to a lightly floured surface. Knead until smooth and elastic, about 5 minutes. With lightly floured hands, shape dough into a ball, then flatten into a 7-inch disk. Press olives into top of loaf. Set on a lightly floured baking sheet. Let rise in a warm place for 1½ hours or until doubled in volume. Preheat oven to 400°. Bake bread 45 minutes or until it sounds hollow when tapped on the bottom. Transfer to a rack. Let cool slightly before serving.

SWEET POTATO ROLLS

Yields: 24 servings

2 packages yeast
¼ cup sugar
½ cup warm water
3 tablespoons butter, melted
1 tablespoon salt

3 eggs
3 cups flour
½ cup cooked mashed sweet potatoes
2 tablespoons heavy cream

Preheat oven to 375°. In a bowl combine yeast with 1 tablespoon sugar and warm water, let sit 5 minutes. Add remaining sugar, butter, salt, and 2 eggs to yeast mixture, stir to blend well. Stir in 3 cups of flour, 1 cup at a time, then stir in sweet potatoes. Turn out onto a floured surface and knead 2-3 minutes, adding small handfuls of additional flour as needed to prevent dough from sticking to the board. When dough is smooth and springy, shape into a ball. Place in an oiled bowl and coat dough completely with oil. Cover bowl with plastic wrap and let sit in a warm place until doubled in size, about 1 hour.

Punch down dough and shape into 2-dozen golf ball-sized balls. Place them on a buttered cookie sheet about 2 inches apart. Cover and let rise until doubled in size.

Beat egg and heavy cream. Brush rolls with this mixture. Bake 20 minutes.

SOFT PRETZELS

Yields: 12 pretzels

1 package dry yeast
1½ cups warm water
1 teaspoon sugar
1 teaspoon salt

3½ cups flour
1 egg beaten for egg wash
Kosher salt

Preheat oven to 425°. Dissolve yeast in water and sugar, allow to sit 5 minutes. Add salt and 2 cups flour. Beat with a wooden spoon until smooth. Add remaining flour and knead until smooth and easy to handle, about 5 minutes. Place in a greased bowl, cover and let rise until doubled in size. Cut dough into 12 equal pieces, shape into pretzel shapes and place on a greased pan. Brush with egg and sprinkle with kosher salt. Bake 15-20 minutes or until soft and golden. Best eaten fresh.

Recipe can easily be doubled.

Kid's Pick

On Shabbat, the manna
looked shinier and had an even
better smell and taste.

WATER CHALLAH

Yields: 2 loaves

3 cups warm water
4 teaspoons dry yeast (2 packets
    or 1 rounded tablespoon)
½ cup sugar
3 cups flour

1 tablespoon salt
⅓ cup light olive oil
5-6 cups flour
1 egg
1 tablespoon cold water

Preheat oven to 350°. In a large bowl, 20-cup food processor or 6-quart mixer, mix 3 cups water, yeast and sugar. Let sit 5-10 minutes. Add 3 cups flour and mix. Add salt and oil and mix. Add 5-6 cups flour, mix and knead. Place in oiled bowl or bag, turn dough over to lightly coat with oil on both sides. Cover. Let rise 2-4 hours or until doubled in size. Divide dough in half. Separate each half of dough into 3 equal portions and make ropes. Braid into loaves and tie off ends. Place on parchment paper for easiest clean-up or on a cookie sheet sprinkled with cornmeal or flour. Paint with egg wash (1 egg mixed with 1 tablespoon water). Let rise 45-90 minutes. Bake 30-45 minutes, until as golden or brown as you like it.

Best when fresh and served immediately.

WHOLE WHEAT BREAD

Yields: 2 loaves

2 (¼-ounce) packages dry yeast
½ teaspoon sugar
½ cup warm water
⅓ cup honey
¼ cup shortening

1 tablespoon salt
1¾ cups water
3 cups whole-wheat flour
3½ cups white flour
1 egg for egg wash

Preheat oven to 325°. Dissolve yeast and sugar in warm water. Let sit 5 minutes. Blend honey and shortening together and gradually add yeast mix, salt, water and whole-wheat flour. Gradually add white flour, kneading until smooth and elastic. Cover and let rise until doubled in size, 45-60 minutes. Shape into 2 loaves and let rise again until doubled in size, 45-60 minutes. Brush loaves with beaten egg. Bake 30-40 minutes until golden and sounds hollow when tapped on bottom. Recipe can easily be doubled.

Best eaten fresh, since there are no eggs or preservatives in recipe.

On Shabbat, we lay a white tablecloth, lay the challot on top of that, and place a covering atop the challot, representing the two layers of dew that protected the manna.

WHOLE GRAIN CHALLAH

Yields: 4 (1-pound) challahs

¼ cup warm water
1 cup plus 1 tablespoon sugar or honey
1 (¼ ounce) yeast packet
1 cup water
1 cup soy, oat or rice milk
    (any type will do)
½ cup oil

1 teaspoon salt
Gluten, follow directions on box,
    optional
6-8 cups flour
    (wheat, oat, barley or rye)
2 tablespoons flax seeds

Preheat oven to 325°. Combine warm water, 1 tablespoon sugar or honey, and yeast and let stand 10 minutes. Add water, milk, remaining sugar or honey, oil, salt, gluten, flour and flax seeds. Mix and knead until firm and sticky (it is best to start with 6 cups flour and slowly add until desired consistency). Let stand 1-2 hours. Shape and let stand 1 hour. Bake about 35 minutes.

The mix of flour should suit everyone's personal tastes; bread flour can be added to the mix. Gluten makes the bread texture softer; for a heavier bread, leave out. Dough can be prepared in advance and frozen. It doesn't take up a lot of freezer space. When baked, it tastes like it was freshly made.

PITA BREAD

Yields: 6-8 servings

1 package (2¼ teaspoons) dry yeast
1 teaspoon sugar
1 cup warm water

2 tablespoons olive oil
½ teaspoon salt
2 cups flour

Dissolve yeast and sugar in warm water. Let sit 5 minutes. Add olive oil, salt and flour and knead until smooth. Let rise in a covered oiled bowl until doubled in size. Preheat oven to 500°. Put an inverted cookie sheet in oven and let heat. Roll out dough in pita shapes and place on hot cookie sheet for about 1 minute until puffed and high. Allow to cool slightly, serve warm.

Recipe can easily be doubled or tripled.

Cornmeal-Rye Bread

Yields: 2 loaves

¾ cup stone ground cornmeal
1 tablespoon molasses
1 tablespoon sugar
2 teaspoons fennel seeds
1 tablespoon anise seeds
1 teaspoon caraway seeds
1¼ cups boiling water

1 cup milk
1 tablespoon salt
1½ tablespoons dry yeast
¾ cup rye flour
5 cups white flour
¾ cup dried currants or raisins

The night before, mix cornmeal, molasses, sugar, fennel seeds, anise seeds and caraway seeds. Pour boiling water over and mix in. Cover with a plate and leave overnight. The following day, mix in milk, salt, yeast and rye flour. Then add white flour 1 cup at a time and then ½ cup at a time, until a sticky dough is formed that pulls away from the sides of the bowl. Turn out onto a kneading surface floured with ½ cup white flour. Knead flour in until the dough is just stiff enough to knead properly. Knead 10-15 minutes until dough is smooth and elastic. It will remain a little sticky. Form into a ball.

Lightly oil a large bowl. Place the ball of dough in it and turn dough to coat it with oil on all sides. Cover and set in a warm, draft-free place until doubled in bulk.

Punch dough down and turn out. Cut in half, roll out each half. Sprinkle with raisins or currants. Roll up the 2 halves and shape into two loaves. Let loaves rest a few minutes while you spray two 8½ x 4½ x 2½-inch bread pans. Dust pans with cornmeal, place the loaves in them, cover and set to rise again until almost doubled in bulk or until tops are rounded above the rims of the pans.

Preheat oven to 425°. Brush tops of loaves with water, and cut 1 or 2 slashes into them with a razor blade or very sharp knife. Bake about 10 minutes. Lower temperature to 350° and continue baking about 20 minutes or until tops sound hollow when rapped with a wooden spoon. Turn out of pans and bake for a few more minutes directly on oven rack. Remove to cool on a rack. Do not slice until thoroughly cool, preferably the next day.

This bread is excellent toasted for breakfast, or, notwithstanding that the recipe seems like it will produce an excessively sweet loaf, thinly sliced for sandwiches

Variations: For pareve loaves, substitute soy milk for milk. Spice proportions are a matter of personal preference. Caraway seeds can be omitted or increased. If the latter, taste will be more like that commonly associated with rye bread. The proportion of rye flour can be varied. Note, though, that dough becomes harder to handle if there is more rye flour. In this recipe, as in most, the raisins or currants can be soaked for ½ hour in brandy or bourbon.

Prepare Ahead of Time

Breads

Classic Cinnamon Rolls

Yields: 12 servings

ROLLS

¼ cup milk	¼ cup warm water
¼ cup sugar	2¼ cups all-purpose flour
½ teaspoon salt	1 egg
6 tablespoons butter	¼ cup brown sugar, firmly packed
1 package dry yeast	½ teaspoon ground cinnamon

GLAZE

1 cup powdered sugar, sifted	2 tablespoons milk

Combine milk, sugar, salt and 3 tablespoons of butter in a saucepan over low to medium heat until butter melts. Allow to cool, but only until very warm (105°-115°, if you have a thermometer).

Dissolve yeast in warm water in a large mixing bowl; let stand 5 minutes. Stir in milk mixture, 1½ cups flour, and egg. Beat with electric mixer at medium speed until smooth. Stir in remaining ¾ cup flour.

Turn out dough onto lightly floured surface and knead until smooth and elastic, about 8 minutes. Place in a well-greased bowl, turning to coat all sides of the dough. Cover and let rise in a warm place for 1 hour. The dough should rise to almost double in size.

Melt 2 tablespoons of butter. Punch the dough down and turn it onto a lightly floured surface. Roll out into a 12 x 8-inch rectangle. Brush with melted butter. Combine brown sugar and cinnamon and sprinkle over rectangle. Roll up dough, starting at the long side. Pinch the seam to seal it, but do not seal ends. Cut the roll in one-inch slices, placing each slice, cut side down, in greased 8-inch square pan. Melt 1 tablespoon of butter and brush the tops.

Cover again and leave in a warm place to rise 40 minutes. Rolls should rise some, but will not double. Preheat oven to 350°. Bake 35 minutes. To make glaze, combine powdered sugar and milk, stirring well. Drizzle over warm rolls and serve.

These can also be made the night before. Just after brushing the tops, let them rise in the refrigerator. Then bake in the morning.

Spreads *and* Dips

The manna's taste was that of a "Tsapichit B'dvash," two thin wafers with honey spread in-between.

(Da'as Mikrah, Parshas B'shalach)

CREAMY GARLIC DIP

Yields: 1 cup

8 ounces cream cheese
1 bunch cilantro

4 large garlic cloves
Salt and pepper to taste

Blend all ingredients in blender until smooth. Serve immediately or chill until ready to serve.

Serve on baked potatoes or fried eggplant. Can mix with tuna fish. Also tastes good with low fat cream cheese.

HERB CHEESE SPREAD

Yields: 3 cups

2 (8-ounce) packages cream cheese, softened
8 ounces unsalted whipped butter, softened
¼ teaspoon garlic powder
½ teaspoon salt

½ teaspoon dried basil
½ teaspoon dried marjoram
½ teaspoon dried chives
¼ teaspoon dried thyme
1 teaspoon dried dill
Pepper to taste

Combine all ingredients and mix with an electric mixer until well blended. Chill several hours. Serve with challah, crackers, or toast points.

Keeps well in the refrigerator.

QUICK SALMON SPREAD

Yields: 6-8 servings

1 (7¾-ounce) can salmon, drained
1 (8-ounce) package cream cheese,
    softened
½ small onion, grated

1 tablespoon lemon juice
1 teaspoon red horseradish
¾ cup chopped nuts, optional

Mix all ingredients together and serve immediately or chill until ready to serve.

BLUE CHEESE BALL

Yields: 16 servings

1 (8-ounce) package cream cheese
8 ounces blue cheese
½ cup butter

1 tablespoon fresh lemon juice
2 tablespoons chopped onions
1 tablespoon paprika

Mix all ingredients, except paprika, and roll into a ball. Sprinkle with paprika. Serve with favorite crackers.

Let ingredients sit out for a while before preparing to make mixing easier. Use half recipe for a small party or potluck.

A strong blue cheese will do well in this recipe because it's somewhat diluted by the cream cheese.

LIPTAUER CHEESE

Yields: 1½ cups

1 green onion, chopped
2 tablespoons finely chopped chives
1 tablespoon capers, drained
1 tablespoon paprika
1 teaspoon caraway seeds
1 teaspoon dry mustard

¼ teaspoon salt
2 teaspoons freshly ground black
   pepper
1 (8-ounce) package cream cheese,
   softened
⅓ cup unsalted butter, softened

In a food processor, combine green onion, chives, capers, paprika, caraway seeds, mustard, salt and pepper. Run 15 seconds, or until ingredients are reduced to a thick paste. Add cream cheese and butter and process another 20 seconds, or until smooth. Scrape down sides and run until smooth. Serve immediately or refrigerate.

Black Bean Hummus

Yields: 2 cups

6 garlic cloves
1 (15-ounce) can chickpeas (garbanzo
　　beans), drained and rinsed
1 (15-ounce) can black beans, drained
　　and rinsed

1 cup tahini
⅓ cup fresh lemon juice
Salt to taste

Place garlic cloves in food processor and process until finely chopped. Add chickpeas and black beans with tahini and lemon juice until completely processed and combined. Add salt to taste. Cover and refrigerate until ready to use. Serve with pita wedges or crudités.

No-Fail Hummus

Yields: 3 cups

2 (14-ounce) cans chickpeas
2 tablespoons tahini
2 tablespoons lemon juice
1 tablespoon chopped garlic
1 teaspoon salt

1½ tablespoons ground cumin
½ teaspoon pepper
2 tablespoons extra virgin olive oil
Paprika, to taste

Place all ingredients except olive oil and paprika in food processor. Process until smooth, drizzling in olive oil as the processor runs. Taste to see if it needs more garlic, lemon juice or seasoning. Adjust as necessary. Sprinkle with paprika when done.

FETA AND SUN-DRIED TOMATO DIP

Yields: 1½-2 cups

1 (8-ounce) jar sun-dried tomatoes,
    drained
⅓ cup fresh basil
1 tablespoon extra virgin olive oil

2-3 garlic cloves
1 (6-ounce) package feta cheese
⅓ cup dry white wine

Preheat oven to 350°. Finely chop tomatoes in a food processor and add basil, olive oil and garlic. Chop all together. Add feta and mix by hand. Add white wine. Put in an oven safe dish and bake 20-30 minutes or until done.

Makes a tasty spinach salad when all ingredients are mixed (not cooked) together and added to spinach leaves.

CANDIED BRIE

Yields: 12-15 servings

1 (8-ounce) wheel Brie cheese
¼ cup dark brown sugar

1½ cups pecan halves
    (or more to cover top of Brie)
¼ cup coffee liqueur

Remove rind from top of Brie. Spread brown sugar over top of Brie to cover and press pecan halves into brown sugar. Drizzle coffee liqueur over top. Microwave 30-45 seconds until soft.

Serve with crackers or fresh fruits, such as cantaloupes, apples, pears and strawberries.

The Jewish people have always liked salty foods. Herring and lox are both very popular dishes among Jews of Eastern European descent.

Chopped Herring

Yields: 2 cups

1 small jar herring tidbits
3 tablespoons chopped onion
½ cup peeled, chopped apple
2 eggs, hard-boiled

3 tablespoons cider vinegar
2 slices white bread, crusts trimmed
1 teaspoon sugar
2 tablespoons salad oil

Combine herring, onion, apple, and eggs and together. Pour vinegar over bread and add to herring mixture with sugar and oil. Chop until very smooth. Taste for seasoning; add more vinegar if needed. Chill.

Baba Ganouj

Yields: 4 cups

1 (3-pound) eggplant
2 teaspoons minced fresh garlic
½ cup tahini

2 tablespoons fresh lemon juice
1 teaspoon salt

Roast eggplant on grill or on top of gas burner until skin is silvery and charred and fork-tender. Allow to cool, then slit eggplant lengthwise and use a spoon to scoop out pulp. Place in a large bowl. Break up eggplant and add other ingredients. Mix completely, taste to adjust seasonings. Cool. Serve with pita bread, crackers or crudités.

If using an electric oven, roast in oven at 350° until skin is charred, 45 minutes to an hour. Roasting eggplant imparts a smoky flavor that is essential. Roasting on stovetop is messy but well worth it.

Use care to avoid bits of blackened eggplant skin, as this will impart a bitter taste. You can also put all ingredients into food processor and pulse until smooth.

Hot Artichoke Dip

Yields: 3 cups

1 (12-ounce) can artichoke hearts, drained and chopped
1 cup mayonnaise
½ cup grated Parmesan cheese

1 teaspoon Worcestershire sauce
½ teaspoon garlic powder
2 dashes hot sauce

Preheat oven to 350°. Combine ingredients and pour into a bake-and-serve dish. Bake 20 minutes or until brown on top. Mix, and bake additional 10 minutes or until hot. Serve with baked pita chips or crackers.

Spreads and Dips

In the years of "tzena" — rationing — in the new state of Israel, "mock" delicacies were innovated, such as "chopped liver" from eggplant.

EGGPLANT SPREAD
Yields: 8 servings

2 eggplants
Olive oil for cooking
1 tablespoon lemon juice

2 garlic cloves
Salt and pepper to taste

Slice eggplant into ¼-inch rounds. Fry slices in olive oil over medium-high heat until very brown on each side. Drain slices on brown bag or paper towel. Slice into quarters. Mix with lemon juice, garlic, salt and pepper. Let sit in refrigerator for better flavor.

Good for Passover, a great spread atop matzo. Add cayenne for a little spice.

BLACK BEAN DIP

Yields: 4 cups

2 (15-ounce) cans black beans
1-2 tablespoons oil, preferably olive
1 large onion, chopped
1 green pepper, chopped
2 garlic cloves, crushed

1½ teaspoons ground cumin
1½ teaspoons ground coriander
½ teaspoon salt
¼ teaspoon pepper

Drain beans, reserving liquid. In a large skillet, heat oil. Add onion, green pepper and garlic. Sauté until soft. Add cumin, coriander, salt and pepper. Mix well. Add beans, mashing somewhat with back of spoon. Add reserved liquid as needed for desired consistency while cooking 15-20 minutes. Serve hot or cold with tortilla chips.

EDAMAME HUMMUS

Yields: 8-10 servings

½ pound frozen shelled edamame
¼ cup tahini
⅛ cup water
3 tablespoons lemon juice
1 garlic clove, smashed

¾ teaspoon kosher salt
½ teaspoon ground cumin
¼ teaspoon ground coriander
4 tablespoons extra virgin olive oil
1 tablespoon chopped fresh parsley

Boil beans in salted water 4-5 minutes. In a food processor, purée the edamame, tahini, water, lemon juice, garlic, salt, cumin and coriander until smooth. As it purées, slowly drizzle in 2 tablespoons of olive oil until absorbed. Turn off processor. Stir in parsley and drizzle with remaining oil. Refrigerate 1 hour.

A healthy alternative to guacamole, and it is a prettier green color!

THREE-CHEESE SPREAD WITH CRANBERRIES AND PISTACHIOS

Yields: 8-10 servings

1 (8-ounce) package cream cheese, softened
½ cup butter, softened
2 ounces crumbled blue cheese

4 ounces Brie cheese, rind removed
8 ounces dried cranberries
8 ounces pistachio nuts, chopped

Hold back 1 tablespoon of cranberries and 1 tablespoon of pistachios for garnish. Line a 9-inch cake pan or other mold with plastic wrap. Set aside. In a medium bowl with an electric mixer, beat cream cheese, butter, blue cheese and Brie until smooth. Spread ⅓ of cheese mixture in bottom of mold. Spread cranberries and pistachios on top. Continue layering, ending with cranberries and pistachios. Chill several hours or overnight. Unmold and garnish with reserved cranberries and pistachios.

Serve with ginger snaps or spice wafers.

Appetizers

When the Jews first saw manna, they exclaimed "man hu," meaning "prepared food." They thought it to be an appetizer, a spiritual food to whet their appetite for a "real" meal. They had no idea that such a spiritual substance could be a "real food"!

(Binah L'itim #43)

Just a Reminder…
green = pareve   red = meat   blue = dairy

Soy Good Wings

Yields: 12-15 servings

½ cup water
1 cup soy sauce
1 cup brown or white sugar
¼ cup pineapple juice

¾ cup peanut oil
1 teaspoon grated fresh ginger
1 teaspoon garlic powder
20-24 chicken wings, cut in half

Mix all ingredients except chicken in blender or food processor. Pour over wings and marinate 1 hour. Preheat oven to 350°. Bake in an oven-safe dish 50-60 minutes. Baste while cooking. Serve promptly.

It's also easy to make a dipping sauce. Make extra sauce and reserve part. Bring to a boil in small pan and simmer 5 minutes.

Great for the gang on football Sundays!

Chickpeas have long been a Jewish favorite. Ashkenazim eat them with black pepper, and Sephardim add them to various dishes like rice, couscous and soup.

SNACKIN' PEAS

Yields: 4 servings

1 (15-ounce) can chickpeas
Vegetable cooking spray
1 teaspoon olive oil

Pinch of salt
1 teaspoon store-bought seasonings, preferably southwestern

Preheat oven to 450°. Rinse and drain chickpeas, spread out on a baking sheet greased with cooking spray. Cover with foil and bake 10-15 minutes. Gently shake chickpeas on pan in oven every 3-5 minutes to bake evenly and prevent browning too quickly. Remove when golden brown and place in bowl while hot. Stir in olive oil and salt. Sprinkle with seasoning. Cool 3-5 minutes.

These could also be seasoned with fivespice powder, cayenne pepper, or falafel seasoning.

MARINATED 'SHROOMS

Yields: 12 servings

8 ounces white button mushrooms
½ cup olive oil
¼ cup balsamic vinegar

1 teaspoon salt
2 garlic cloves, crushed
Fresh cracked pepper, to taste

Cut mushrooms into thick slices. Mix remaining ingredients in a plastic bowl with tightly-fitting cover. Place mushrooms in bowl, cover, and shake. Set aside at least 2 hours.

This makes a fantastic appetizer. Serve with crackers and cheese or toasted French bread.

COWBOY BEEF STRIPS

Yields: Depends on portions used

Top round steak, cut very thin
Liquid smoke

Seasoned salt
Fresh ground pepper

Brush liquid smoke on each slice of steak (both sides). Sprinkle with seasoned salt and a generous amount of pepper. Cover and refrigerate overnight. Spread directly on oven racks at lowest temperature until dry and crispy, about 4-6 hours.

For ease of slicing, freeze meat, then allow to thaw just slightly.

Prepare Ahead of Time

MEAT ROLL IN PUFF PASTRY

Yields: 4 servings

1 frozen puff pastry sheet, thawed
1 pound ground beef
1 (6-ounce) can tomato sauce
2 tablespoons matzoh meal

1 egg
½ package onion soup mix
2 cubes mushroom soup mix, for sauce

Preheat oven to 350°. Roll out puff pastry sheet. Mix together all other ingredients, except soup cubes. Spread mix over entire sheet. Roll up jelly-roll style, ending with the seam side down. Bake 1 hour. For sauce, follow soup directions but reduce water amount by ½ cup to make sauce consistency. Slice roll into portions and pour 2 tablespoons sauce over each.

In the early part of the 20th century, in places that were home to large Jewish communities of hungry men who came to make their fortune, and later sent for their families, the delicatessen, or deli, flourished.

SWEET AND TANGY MEATBALLS

Yields: 10 servings

MEATBALLS
2 pounds ground beef
2 eggs

½ cup bread crumbs

SAUCE
½ cup light brown sugar
1 cup prepared spaghetti sauce,
    preferably with basil
½ cup water
¼ cup ketchup

1 tablespoon minced onion
1 tablespoon dried parsley
1 teaspoon garlic powder
¼ teaspoon pepper

Preheat oven to 350°. Mix all ingredients for the meatballs. Brown over medium heat and remove fat. Place in an ovenproof baking dish. Mix ingredients for sauce and add to meatballs. Cover and bake 45 minutes. Serve hot.

KREPLACH

Yields: 4 servings

DOUGH
1 egg, beaten   1 cup flour, sifted
¼ teaspoon salt

FILLING
1 cup cooked ground beef   2 tablespoons shortening
2 tablespoons minced onion   1 egg

Dough: Mix ingredients. Dough will be stiff; knead until smooth and elastic. Roll out until paper thin. Cut into 2-inch squares.

Filling: Mix ingredients together. Spread spoonful of filling onto each square of dough. Fold in half and seal. Drop into boiling salted water.

Great in soup. Can also be fried until golden brown or baked on a greased cookie sheet until golden brown.

NUTTY APRICOT BRIE TARTS

Yields: 2 dozen servings

24 pecan halves
1 (8-ounce) package Brie, chilled

⅓ cup apricot preserves
2 packages phyllo cups

Preheat oven to 350°. Bake pecans in shallow pan 3-5 minutes or until toasted. Cool. Remove rind from cheese; cut cheese into 24 cubes, set aside. Spoon ½ teaspoon preserves into each phyllo cup. Top with cheese cube and pecan half. Bake 5 minutes or until cheese melts. Serve immediately.

Great for a wine and cheese party — impresses all the guests!

ASPARAGUS PHYLLO CRISPS

Yields: 36 servings

36 fresh asparagus spears, cleaned, with
    woody ends removed
6 sheets phyllo dough

¼ cup margarine, melted
Salt and pepper, to taste
Parmesan cheese

Preheat oven to 375°. Cut each of the 6 phyllo sheets into 6 squares. Lay squares flat on counter and brush with melted margarine. Add salt, pepper and Parmesan cheese, to taste. Place asparagus sideways on the phyllo square, with the asparagus top and bottom protruding, then roll it up. Place on a greased cookie sheet, leaving a space between each one for better browning. Brush lightly with margarine again. Bake 10-15 minutes, until golden brown.

These can be made the day before. Cover well with plastic wrap and keep refrigerated until just before baking. Do not freeze unbaked.

In Judaism, the round,
perfect egg has always been associated
with the mysteries of life and death, as well
as with fertility and immortality.

SALMON DEVILED EGGS

Yields: 6 servings

6 eggs
1 teaspoon Dijon mustard
4 tablespoons mayonnaise
Pepper, to taste

2 ounces smoked salmon, finely diced
1 tablespoon finely diced red onion
Salt, to taste
Fresh dill, finely chopped, for topping

Place eggs in a saucepan and cover with cold water. Bring to a boil and boil 11 minutes. Immediately drain eggs and shock them in an ice cold water bath to stop the cooking process. Let cool 10 minutes. Peel, dry and cut eggs lengthwise. Scoop out hard yolk into mixing bowl. Reserve whites for stuffing.

Mix egg yolks, mustard and mayonnaise, add pepper to taste. Add salmon and red onion. Add salt to taste, continue stirring until mixture is a creamy consistency. Fill small-tip pastry bag with mixture and pipe into egg whites. Sprinkle with fresh dill.

DRUNKEN MUSHROOMS

Yields: 1 dozen

12 large mushrooms
1 onion, chopped
4 large garlic cloves, chopped
½ teaspoon salt
½ teaspoon pepper

¼ cup chopped fresh parsley
½ cup grated mozzarella cheese
1 tablespoon grated Parmesan cheese
2-3 tablespoons whiskey
2 tablespoons olive oil

Preheat oven to 350°. Wash mushrooms thoroughly and scoop out stem and flesh, saving for later. Leave mushroom shells as thin as possible without damaging them. Sauté onion in oil over low heat, then briefly add garlic (do not brown). Chop scooped-out mushroom meat, add to onion and garlic and sauté until most of the mushroom liquid evaporates. Add salt, pepper and parsley. Sauté 5 more minutes. Add cheeses and whiskey. Pour olive oil into 9 x 13 x 2-inch glass baking dish. Fill mushrooms with mixture and place in pan. Bake 20-30 minutes.

STUFFED MUSHROOMS

Yields: 20 servings

40 large fresh mushrooms, about
    1 pound
½ cup freshly grated Parmesan cheese
½ cup dry bread crumbs
½ cup grated onion
2 garlic cloves, minced

2 tablespoons chopped fresh parsley
½ teaspoon salt
¼ teaspoon pepper
½ teaspoon dried oregano
½ cup butter, melted

Preheat oven to 350°. Grease cookie sheet. Clean mushrooms and remove stems. Chop stems and place in a medium-size bowl with Parmesan cheese, bread crumbs, onion, garlic, parsley, salt, pepper and oregano. Mix well. Place mushroom caps on greased cookie sheet and fill with bread crumb mixture. Drizzle melted butter over mushrooms and bake until golden brown, about 20-25 minutes. Serve hot.

DEVILED SALMON CAKES

Yields: 1 dozen

3 (6-ounce) cans boneless salmon,
    drained
4 eggs, beaten
½ cup mayonnaise
½ cup finely diced onion
½ cup finely diced celery

½ cup frozen corn kernels, thawed
1½ tablespoons Dijon mustard
2 teaspoons sweet pickle relish
1½ cups crushed saltines
Dash Worcestershire sauce, to taste
Olive oil

Mix together salmon, eggs and mayonnaise until well blended. Add remaining ingredients. Mix together well. Form into 1½-inch patties. Heat oil on medium-high heat. Place patties in frying pan and flatten with fork. Sauté in oil over medium heat until brown, flip and finish browning.

This is an easy recipe to double. You can also make larger patties to serve as entrées.

SPICY TUNA ROLLS

Yields: 1 dozen

1 pound fresh (sushi grade) tuna, diced
3 tablespoons chopped fresh chives
¼ cup soy sauce
2 tablespoons sesame oil

2 tablespoons rice wine vinegar
2 cucumbers
Black sesame seeds, for topping

SAUCE
¼ cup mayonnaise

1 teaspoon chili paste

Marinate tuna in chives, soy sauce, sesame oil and vinegar about 1 hour in refrigerator. Peel cucumbers and slice lengthwise as thinly as possible. Place small portion of tuna on cucumber slice and roll up. Thoroughly mix mayonnaise and chili paste. Put dollop of sauce on top and sprinkle with sesame seeds. Serve immediately or refrigerate.

Tuna Wontons
with Asian Guacamole

Yields: 24 servings

2 pounds fresh tuna
Wonton wrappers
1 large avocado, mashed
1 teaspoon wasabi
1 small shallot, diced

Juice of 1 lime
Salt and pepper, to taste
Garlic, to taste
Fresh ginger, thinly sliced

Preheat oven to 350°. Spray a mini-muffin tin with vegetable spray. Spray wonton wrappers with vegetable spray and season with salt and pepper. Bake in muffin tins until golden, about 10 minutes.

Combine avocado, wasabi, shallot, lime, salt and pepper to make guacamole. Refrigerate.

Season tuna with salt, pepper and garlic. Grill or broil 1 minute on each side; should still be rare in center. Cut into ¼-inch slices. Put 1 slice of fresh ginger in bottom of each wonton cup. Add spoonful of guacamole. Top with slice of tuna. Serve immediately.

SPANIKOPITAS

Yields: 16-18 servings

1 (17¼-ounce) package frozen puff
    pastry sheets
1 (10-ounce) package frozen chopped
    spinach, thawed and well drained
2 eggs, beaten
½ cup crumbled feta cheese

1 medium onion, finely chopped
2 tablespoons chopped fresh parsley
1 teaspoon salt
½ teaspoon pepper
1 egg beaten with 1 teaspoon water

Thaw pastry 20-30 minutes. Preheat oven to 400°. On a floured board, roll each pastry sheet to a 12-inch square. Cut into 16 3-inch squares. Combine spinach, eggs, cheese, onion, parsley, salt and pepper. Spoon mixture into center of squares. Brush egg wash around edges of one half of pastry. Fold pastry over filling to form triangle; seal edges. Place on ungreased baking sheet and brush tops with egg wash. Bake 20 minutes or until golden brown.

ITALIAN SPINACH BALLS

Yields: 60 spinach balls

2 (10-ounce) packages frozen chopped
    spinach
2 cups seasoned bread crumbs
1 large onion, grated
4 eggs, beaten

½ cup grated Parmesan cheese
¾ cup margarine, melted
1½ teaspoons dried thyme
½ teaspoon garlic salt
¼ teaspoon pepper

Cook spinach according to package directions. Squeeze out all liquid. Mix by hand with remaining ingredients.

Chill at least 2 hours (can be chilled overnight and rolled the next day). Roll into 1-inch balls. Place on greased cookie sheet. Preheat oven to 350°. Bake until outside is crispy and bubbly, 10-15 minutes.

Serve warm, with sweet hot mustard.

Spinach balls may be shaped, frozen on cookie sheets until hard (uncooked), and then transferred into freezer bags. Defrost before baking.

Prepare Ahead of Time

FALAFEL PITAS WITH GOAT CHEESE SAUCE

Yields: 4 servings

FALAFEL
1 cup dried chickpeas
½ cup chopped green onions
½ cup chopped fresh parsley
1 teaspoon baking powder
1 teaspoon ground coriander
1 teaspoon ground cumin
½ teaspoon salt
¼ teaspoon baking soda
¼ teaspoon black pepper
¼ teaspoon cayenne pepper
1 (6-inch) whole wheat pita, torn into large pieces
2 garlic cloves, chopped
3 large egg whites
Cooking spray

RELISH
2 cups chopped seeded plum tomatoes
1 cup chopped seeded English cucumbers
¼ cup chopped green onions
1 tablespoon chopped fresh parsley
1 tablespoon lemon juice
1 Serrano chile, minced

SAUCE
1 cup plain low-fat yogurt
2 ounces soft (log style) goat cheese
⅛ teaspoon salt
1 small garlic clove, minced
4 (6-inch) whole wheat pitas, halved

Preheat oven to 350°.

Falafel: Sort and wash chickpeas and place in a large bowl. Cover with water to 2 inches above chickpeas, cover bowl and let stand 8 hours or overnight. Drain. Combine ingredients, except egg whites, in food processor, pulse 8-10 times until finely chopped. Spoon mixture into a bowl. Add egg whites to chickpea mixture and stir well. Let stand 15 minutes. Divide mixture into 16 equal portions, shaping each into a ½-inch thick patty. Place patties on baking sheet coated with cooking spray. Bake 10 minutes or until lightly browned.

Relish: Combine all ingredients.

Sauce: Combine yogurt, goat cheese, salt and garlic, stirring with whisk until smooth.

Place 2 falafel patties in each pita half, spoon about ⅓ cup relish and 2½ tablespoons sauce into each. Serve immediately.

Prepare Ahead of Time

SALMON MOUSSE CHEESECAKE

Yields: 12 servings

1 cup grated Parmesan cheese
1 cup soft bread crumbs
½ cup butter, melted
1 tablespoon olive oil
1 cup chopped onion
½ cup chopped red bell pepper
½ cup chopped green bell pepper

Freshly ground black pepper, to taste
1¾ pounds cream cheese, room
    temperature
4 eggs
½ cup heavy cream
1 cup grated smoked Gouda cheese
2 cups chopped smoked salmon

Preheat oven to 350°. In a small bowl, combine Parmesan, bread crumbs and butter. Press into bottom of a greased 9-inch springform pan. In a medium skillet, sauté onions and bell peppers in olive oil. Add pepper to taste.

Beat cream cheese with eggs in a large bowl until foamy, about 4 minutes. Beat in cream, Gouda, sautéed vegetables, and smoked salmon until well mixed. Pour into springform pan. Bake about 75 minutes. Allow to cool to room temperature before serving.

WORTH THE EFFORT

DOLMADES

Yields: 10-12 servings

1 pound ground beef	2 teaspoons finely chopped fresh mint
1 pound ground lamb	½ teaspoon salt
¾ cup basmati rice, uncooked	1 teaspoon pepper
⅓ cup finely chopped Vidalia onion	1 egg
2 teaspoons finely chopped fresh cilantro	Grape leaves

Cook rice according to package instructions. Mix all ingredients together in a large mixing bowl, except grape leaves.

Roll the meat mix, about 1½ tablespoons at a time, into the grape leaves. Roll the leaves over the meat and tuck in both ends. Place rolls in a pot, tightly together. Add enough cold water to cover the rolls, but not by much. Place a weight, such as a smaller pot lid, on top of the rolls to keep them submerged. Bring water to a gentle boil. Boil 45 minutes. Remove immediately from the pot, and serve either hot or cold. May be drizzled with fresh lemon juice and extra virgin olive oil.

SPECIAL GRAPE LEAF PREPARATION INSTRUCTIONS

If you are using fresh grape leaves, just cut the stem from the leaves, and use the leaf.

If using preserved grape leaves (usually preserved in a vinegar or salt brine), you must wash and soak the leaves 5-6 hours. Change water often, and individually rinse them. They are done soaking when they no longer have a salty taste.

Good either cold or hot. You won't have to worry about leftovers!

Prepare Ahead of Time

Soups

The "multitudes of nations" who joined the Jewish people in their 40-year desert experience ate the leftover manna which the sun melted into liquid.

(Zohar II, 192)

Just a Reminder...
green = pareve   red = meat   blue = dairy

ZUCCHINI SOUP

Yields: 8 servings

3 large or 4 medium zucchini, sliced
½ cup chopped onion
¼ cup long-grain rice
Water to cover

4 tablespoons chicken soup powder
1 teaspoon curry powder, optional
1 teaspoon Dijon mustard, optional

In a large pot, combine zucchini, onion, rice, chicken soup powder and enough water to cover zucchini. Bring to a boil, then simmer 15 minutes or until zucchini are tender. Insert immersion blender or purée in blender, adding curry powder and mustard if desired.

If making dairy, add ½-1 cup nonfat yogurt before serving.

This soup is a hit every time, with or without the optional ingredients!

ASPARAGUS BISQUE

Yields: 6 servings

1 pound fresh asparagus
½ large onion, chopped
1 cup chopped celery
2 cups vegetable stock

¼ teaspoon dried marjoram
⅛ teaspoon salt
Pinch white pepper
¼ cup plain, low-fat yogurt

Combine all ingredients except yogurt in a pan and bring to a boil. Cover and simmer 10 minutes. Insert immersion blender or purée in blender. Add yogurt and blend until smooth.

BEEF BARLEY SOUP

Yields: 8-10 servings

2½ pounds stew beef, cut into chunks
1 (14½-ounce) can crushed tomatoes
1 large onion, diced
¾ of (1-pound) package baby carrots

5 stalks celery
Salt and pepper, to taste
1 cup medium barley, washed

Place tomatoes in a large soup pot with meat, onions, carrots, celery and seasonings. Add water up to at least 2 inches from top of pan. Remove celery when soup is almost done. Dice celery and put back in soup if you wish. Let mixture come to a boil and simmer 15 minutes. Add barley. Make sure liquid is not too close to the top and then cover. Cook over medium heat 1½-2 hours. Stir occasionally.

A meal unto itself. Serve with bread or dinner rolls.

CREAMY MUSHROOM SOUP

Yields: 8 servings

4 tablespoons olive oil
3 pounds mushrooms, washed and
    chopped
1 small onion
1 garlic clove, pressed

4 cubes mushroom or chicken bouillon
6 cups water
Dash of coriander
Dash of hot sauce
Salt, to taste

Sauté mushrooms, onion and garlic in olive oil over medium heat until all ingredients are soft. Add bouillon, water, coriander and hot sauce. Bring to a boil. Stir to mix ingredients. Allow to simmer 10 minutes. Cool 10 minutes. Insert immersion blender or purée in blender. Reheat slowly. Salt to taste.

BLACK BEAN SOUP

Yields: 6 servings

2 tablespoons vegetable oil
1 onion, chopped
3 garlic cloves, chopped
1 teaspoon cumin

3 teaspoons chili powder
½ teaspoon oregano
3 (15-ounce) cans black beans
Black pepper to taste

In a large pot, sauté onion in oil for 5 minutes over medium heat. Stir in garlic, cumin, chili powder and oregano. Purée one can of beans and add to pot. Drain liquid from second can and add beans to pot. Add remaining can of beans with liquid to pot. Reduce heat and simmer 15 minutes, stirring often. Add black pepper to taste.

Can be served with topping of shredded cheese and/or crumbled tortilla chips.

POTATO LEEK SOUP

Yields: 8 servings

1 teaspoon olive oil
5½ cups diced potatoes
2 cups diced leeks
2 cups diced celery

2 teaspoons minced fresh garlic
1 teaspoon chopped fresh thyme
7 cups vegetable stock
Salt and pepper, to taste

Heat a large pot over high heat. Add olive oil, potatoes, leeks, celery, garlic and thyme. Sauté about 5 minutes, stirring continuously.

Add vegetable stock and bring to a boil. Reduce heat and simmer 15-20 minutes or until potatoes are soft and falling apart. Insert immersion blender or purée in blender until smooth. Season to taste and reheat.

Fresh Pea Soup

Yields: 8½ servings

2 cups chicken stock
3 cups green peas, fresh or frozen
¼ teaspoon white pepper
⅛ teaspoon salt

1 teaspoon sweetener
1 cup soy milk
⅓ cup sherry

Combine all ingredients except soy milk and sherry in a pan and bring to a boil.

Reduce heat, cover and simmer 3-5 minutes. Insert immersion blender or purée in blender. Add soy milk and sherry and blend until smooth. Reheat as necessary.

Ribollita

Yields: 4 servings

1 tablespoon extra virgin olive oil
½ cup chopped onion
⅓ cup chopped celery
⅓ cup sliced carrot
1 garlic clove, finely chopped
1 (19-ounce) can white kidney beans
    (cannelloni), rinsed and drained

1¾ cups chicken broth
1 (14½-ounce) can plum tomatoes with
    juice
2 cups chopped Savoy cabbage
¼ cup diced red bell pepper
¼ cup diced zucchini
⅛ teaspoon dried thyme

Heat olive oil in a large saucepan. Add onion, celery, carrot and garlic. Sauté over low heat until tender, about 5 minutes. Add remaining ingredients and simmer uncovered until vegetables are tender and flavors blended, about 20 minutes.

Though originally a classic Ashkenazi food, today's variety of chicken soup might include a spoonful of hot and spicy zhoug, which is a Yemenite sauce.

CHICKEN SOUP

Yields: 12-14 servings

3 stalks celery, cut into 2-inch pieces
3 carrots cut into 2-inch pieces, or
   15 small baby carrots
3 medium onions, quartered

2 teaspoons salt
2 teaspoons pepper
1 pullet, skinned and cut into pieces
½ cup powdered chicken soup mix

Fill a 6-quart pot ¾ full with cold water. Add celery, carrots, onions, salt and pepper and bring to a boil. Add the pullet pieces and bring back to a boil, then turn down to simmer. Add chicken soup mix and simmer 2 hours. Add more pepper and/or chicken soup powder to taste. Remove chicken and strain the soup.

Serve with matzo balls, noodles or by itself.

For a nice variation, take out the cooked carrots, celery and onions and purée them. Add this mixture back to the soup. It will add texture and flavor. If desired, return some of the chicken meat to the soup or add fresh cooked carrots.

Curry Cauliflower Soup

Yields: 8 servings

½ teaspoon olive oil
1 cup diced onion
½ cup diced celery
1 teaspoon fresh garlic, minced
1 tablespoon curry powder
4 cups cauliflower florets and stems
2 cups diced potatoes

2 teaspoons dried thyme
1 bay leaf
2 quarts vegetable stock, low-salt
¼ teaspoon kosher salt
½ teaspoon freshly ground black pepper
¼ teaspoon nutmeg

Heat a large soup pot over high heat and add olive oil. Stir in onions, celery, garlic, curry powder, and cauliflower. Sauté until onions are translucent, 3-5 minutes.

Stir in potatoes, thyme, bay leaf and stock. Bring to a boil. Reduce heat and simmer until potatoes and cauliflower are tender, 20-30 minutes. Remove bay leaf. Insert immersion blender or purée in blender. Blend until smooth. Season with salt, pepper and nutmeg.

GRANDMA'S RUSSIAN BORSCHT

Yields: 4-6 servings

3 chicken breasts, chopped
3 cups water
1 (28-ounce) can tomatoes, chopped
2 cups red cabbage, chopped
1½ cups potatoes, sliced thin

1½ cups beets, sliced thin
1 large carrot, sliced
1 small onion, chopped
2 teaspoons salt
Pepper to taste

Grill or sauté chicken breast 5 minutes on each side or until cooked through. Set aside. Bring water and tomatoes to a slow boil. Add remaining ingredients. Cover and simmer until vegetables are tender, about 10 minutes. Cut chicken into 1-inch strips. Stir into soup and cook 15 minutes on low heat.

Optional topping-chopped fresh tomatoes.

Not your typical borscht.

LEMON SOUP

Yields: 4 servings

6 cups chicken stock
4 garlic cloves, whole, peeled
⅔ cup uncooked long-grain rice
3 eggs

Juice of 2 fresh lemons
1 teaspoon salt
1 teaspoon pepper

In a large stock pot, bring the stock to a boil. Add garlic and rice. Simmer 10-15 minutes until rice is tender. Remove garlic.

Beat eggs with 2 tablespoons lemon juice until foamy. Beat in a small amount of hot stock. Add this mixture to the stock pot, stirring constantly until blended. Remove from heat immediately. Stir in salt, pepper and remaining lemon juice. Serve immediately.

NOT-SO-MELLOW MELON SOUP

Yields: 8 servings

6 cups cantaloupe, peeled and cubed
2 cups cucumber, peeled, seeded and
   sliced
¼ cup honey
½ teaspoon grated lime rind
3 tablespoons lime juice, preferably
   fresh

1 teaspoon jalapeño pepper, seeded
   and minced
1 teaspoon ground cumin
½ teaspoon salt
1 (16-ounce) carton plain fat-free
   yogurt

Combine cantaloupe and cucumber in a blender or food processor. Process until smooth. Pour ½ the mixture into a bowl. Add honey, lime rind, lime juice and jalapeño pepper to blender and process until they blend in smoothly. Add cumin, salt, and yogurt. Process until blended. Add to the mixture in the bowl and stir well.

Though originally
courtly food at the time of the
Ottoman Empire, stuffed grape leaves, zucchini,
eggplant, onions and tomatoes became staples in
common cuisine in the Middle East.

Tomato Soup with Herbs and Feta

Yields: 10 servings

½ teaspoon olive oil
6 garlic cloves, minced
1 white onion, diced
½ cup chopped celery
6 tomatoes, chopped
4 cups vegetable stock or water

1 teaspoon chopped fresh oregano
1 teaspoon chopped fresh thyme
2 teaspoons chopped fresh sage
½ teaspoon kosher salt
½ teaspoon freshly ground black
    pepper
3 tablespoons crumbled feta cheese

Heat a stockpot over high heat and add olive oil. Stir in garlic, onions and celery and cook 5 minutes. Add tomatoes and vegetable stock or water. Bring to a boil then reduce to a simmer. Add oregano and thyme and simmer 5 minutes.

Insert immersion blender or purée in blender, adding sage, kosher salt and pepper. Return to stockpot and bring to a simmer to reheat. Serve hot. Garnish with 1 teaspoon crumbled feta on top of each bowl.

Best when made with fresh, seasonal tomatoes. Also good served cold like gazpacho.

CARROT-GINGER SOUP WITH CURRIED APPLES

Yields: 5 servings

¼ teaspoon olive oil
4 cups chopped carrots
1 cup chopped yellow onion
1 teaspoon minced garlic
1 teaspoon minced fresh ginger
5 cups vegetable stock
1 teaspoon dried thyme

Kosher salt and pepper, to taste
1½ cups peeled diced Granny Smith apples
½ cup diced white onions
1 tablespoon curry powder
1 teaspoon brown sugar
¼ cup currants

Heat olive oil in a medium pot over medium-high heat. Add carrots, yellow onions, garlic and ginger. Cook 2 minutes. Add vegetable stock, thyme, salt and pepper and bring to a boil. Reduce heat and simmer until carrots are soft, about 20 minutes.

While soup simmers, sauté apples and white onions in oil 2 minutes over medium heat. Add curry powder, sugar and currants and sauté 2 minutes. Remove from heat and set aside.

Insert immersion blender or purée in blender. Purée soup until smooth. Return soup to pan and heat to serve. Adjust seasoning with salt and pepper to taste. If soup is too thick, add more stock or water for a creamy consistency.

Ladle soup into a warmed bowl and spoon 2 tablespoons sautéed apple mix into the center.

Serve immediately.

Chicken soup
has long been considered a
cure-all, the Jewish "penicillin." This
is, in fact, substantiated by
scientific research.

CHICKEN RICE SOUP

Yields: 8-10 servings

4 chicken breasts, skin removed
1 cup brown rice
10-12 cups chicken stock
5-6 carrots, peeled and sliced

1 large onion, chopped
3 stalks celery
Celery salt or seasoning salt and pepper
   to taste

Preheat oven to 350°. Rinse chicken breasts and place them in an 8-inch square baking dish with a little water to prevent sticking. Cook 1 hour. Remove, cool, and cut into bite-size pieces, saving any juice left in baking dish. Set aside.

While chicken is baking, prepare rice according to directions, but substitute chicken stock for the amount of water called for on package directions. Add carrots and onions to stock at the same time that rice is added. This may necessitate adding a little more stock than directions indicate.

While rice, carrots and onions are cooking, pour remainder of chicken stock into a large soup pot with the celery stalks. Bring to a boil, turn down heat for about 3 minutes, then turn off burner. Let stock sit until everything else is ready. Remove celery at that time. Add chicken, chicken-flavored rice and carrot mixture, and salt and pepper to taste. Reheat before serving.

CREAMY CARROT SOUP

Yields: 6-8 servings

1 tablespoon mild olive oil
1 medium onion, peeled and diced
    small
2 pounds carrots, peeled and cut up, or
    use pre-cut
1 medium baking potato, peeled and
    cut into pieces

1 (64-ounce) can vegetable stock
2 cups water
2-3 tablespoons dried dill
⅛ teaspoon salt
⅛ teaspoon cinnamon
Pinch each of dried cloves, nutmeg and
    ginger

In a large stockpot, heat oil. Add onions and brown 1 minute (do not burn). Add carrots and potatoes and brown 1-2 minutes to release flavors, stirring constantly. Add stock and water. Add more water until carrots and potatoes are covered well with liquid. Add dill and salt. Bring to a boil. Cover and cook on low simmer 1-1½ hours, until carrots are tender. Insert immersion blender or purée in blender until creamy. Pour back in pot. Add cinnamon, cloves, nutmeg and ginger. Mix well. Warm again if necessary and serve.

Chef's Choice

CURRIED PUMPKIN AND APPLE SOUP

Yields: 6-8 servings

1 teaspoon margarine, melted
2 medium onions, diced
½ cup diced celery
½ cup diced carrots
¼ teaspoon dry ginger
1 teaspoon curry powder
2 cups apple cider
1 quart pareve chicken stock

3 cups pumpkin purée
⅛ teaspoon nutmeg
1 teaspoon sugar
⅓ teaspoon ground cinnamon
½ teaspoon pumpkin pie spice
Salt and pepper, to taste
4 tart apples (Granny Smith)

In a large soup pan, lightly sauté onion, celery and carrots in margarine over low heat. Add ginger and curry powder and lightly sauté 2 minutes longer. Add cider, chicken stock, pumpkin and remaining seasonings; simmer 20 minutes. Peel, core and dice apples. Set some aside some for garnish. In a separate pan, sauté apples until soft. While apples sauté, strain soup through colander, discarding remaining onions, celery and carrots. Add sautéed apples to soup. Season to taste and garnish with fresh diced apples. Best served immediately.

93

GAZPACHO WITH A TWIST

Yields: 28 servings

18 plum tomatoes or
    2 (28-ounce) cans, chopped
    tomatoes, well drained
3 large green peppers
1 large onion
1 bunch celery
4 large cucumbers
6 garlic cloves, crushed
3 quarts Bloody Mary mix

3 tablespoons red wine vinegar
¼ cup olive oil
1 cup pareve beef flavored bouillon
Hot sauce to taste
Worcestershire sauce to taste
Garlic salt to taste
Pepper, to taste
Tomato wedges, for garnish

Core tomatoes and cut into small pieces for food processor. Chop in food processor until nearly liquid, remove to separate bowl. Clean peppers and chop into small pieces in processor; repeat with onion and celery. Peel, seed and hand chop cucumbers into small pieces. Add all chopped ingredients and garlic to Bloody Mary mix, wine vinegar, olive oil and bouillon and mix well. Season with hot sauce, Worcestershire, garlic salt and pepper. Garnish with tomato wedges.

You may also partially blend the soup in a blender or with an immersion blender for a creamier texture. It should be left somewhat chunky, however.

LENTIL AND BROWN RICE SOUP

Yields: 8-10 servings

5 cups chicken stock
3 cups water
1½ cups lentils, picked over and rinsed
1 cup long-grain brown rice
1 (35-ounce) can tomatoes, drained and chopped (reserve juice)
3 carrots, chopped
1 large onion, chopped
1 large stalk celery, chopped

3 large garlic cloves, minced
½ teaspoon dried basil
½ teaspoon thyme
1 bay leaf
½ cup fresh parsley, minced
2 tablespoons cider vinegar
Salt, to taste
Ground pepper, to taste

In a large, heavy saucepan or Dutch oven, combine chicken stock, water, lentils, rice, tomatoes, carrots, onions, celery, garlic, basil, thyme and bay leaf. Bring soup to a boil. Reduce heat, cover and simmer soup, stirring occasionally, 45-55 minutes or until lentils and rice are both tender. Remove and discard bay leaf. Stir in parsley, vinegar, salt and pepper. If necessary, thin soup with additional hot stock, reserved tomato juice or water.

The consumption of spinach in America rose 33% after the debut of "Popeye the Sailor" in 1929, making it the third favorite food after turkey and ice cream.

PURÉED SPINACH SOUP

Yields: 8-12 servings

4 tablespoons light olive oil
10 mushrooms
½ onion
1 carrot
1 medium potato
    (or ½ head cauliflower)
1 garlic clove

⅛ cup white wine
4 cubes pareve chicken bouillon,
    crumbled
6 cups water
1 pound spinach, washed and stemmed
Salt, to taste
Curry powder, to taste

Cut mushrooms, onion, carrot and potato or cauliflower into small pieces and press garlic. Place vegetables and garlic in a pot with oil. Stir and cook over medium heat until softened. Pour in wine and allow to cook a few minutes. Stir in crumbled bouillon cubes. Add water and bring to a boil. Lower to medium heat, continuing to stir. Add spinach and cook until wilted. Remove soup from heat and insert immersion blender or purée in blender. You may have to blend it in batches. Return blended soup to pot and cook over medium heat until heated through. Add salt and curry powder to taste.

SOUTHWEST ZESTY CHICKEN SOUP

Yields: 12 servings

2 boneless, skinless chicken breasts
½ teaspoon olive oil
¼ cup chopped onions
½ cup chopped carrots
1 cup chopped green peppers
½ cup chopped zucchini
½ cup chopped yellow squash
1 teaspoon finely chopped fresh
    oregano
½ teaspoon minced garlic
¼ teaspoon minced jalapeño

6 cups chicken stock
½ teaspoon kosher salt
⅛ teaspoon freshly ground black
    pepper
2 cups finely julienned cabbage
¼ cup chopped green onions
½ cup diced avocado
2 tablespoons finely chopped cilantro,
    optional
Juice of 1 lime

Cook chicken breasts over medium-high heat 5 minutes on each side or until cooked through. Cut each breast into 1-inch thick slices. Set aside.

Heat a medium-size pan over medium-high heat and lightly coat bottom of pan with olive oil. Add onions, carrots, peppers, zucchini, squash, oregano, garlic and jalapeño and sauté 5-7 minutes to soften vegetables. Stir in stock, salt and pepper. Simmer about 10 minutes to finish cooking the vegetables.

Add chicken, cabbage, green onions, avocado, and cilantro, if desired. Simmer 5 minutes. Squeeze in lime juice. Adjust seasoning with salt and fresh ground pepper to taste.

Wild Rice and Wild Mushroom Soup

Yields: 4-6 servings

½ cup raw wild rice
3 cups boiling water
½ teaspoon salt
½ ounce dried wild mushrooms
2 tablespoons unsalted butter
1 yellow onion, finely chopped
1 stalk celery, finely chopped

½ cup dry white wine
¾ pound fresh cremini mushrooms, brushed clean, trimmed and thinly sliced
3 cups vegetable stock
½ cup heavy whipping cream
Salt and pepper, to taste

Rinse wild rice with several changes of water. Drain and put in a pot. Add 2 cups boiling water and ½ teaspoon salt. Bring to a boil. Cover and simmer until water is absorbed. Set aside to cool. Combine dried mushrooms and 1 cup boiling water and set aside about 30 minutes. Separate mushrooms from liquid (which will be used later). Sauté onion and celery in butter until softened. Increase heat to medium-high. Add wine and cook until reduced to about 2 tablespoons. Reduce heat to medium. Add fresh and wild mushrooms. Sauté 15 minutes. Increase heat to medium-high. Add stock and reserved mushroom liquid. Bring to a boil. Reduce heat to medium and cook uncovered until the mushrooms are very soft (about 20 minutes). Add wild rice and cream. Simmer gently 5 minutes. Season with salt and pepper to taste. Ladle the soup into warmed bowls and serve hot, sprinkling with fresh ground white pepper and chopped Italian parsley if desired.

Salads

With the exception of five vegetables – onions, garlic, melons, cucumbers and leeks – the manna would assume both taste and texture of the desired food. With these five, however, only the taste was present.

(Sefer Haparshios, Parshas B'haaloscha)

Just a Reminder...
green = pareve   red = meat   blue = dairy

CRANBERRY RELISH JUBILEE

Yields: 8 servings

1 can cranberry sauce

1 tablespoon grated orange rind

1 cup pitted Bing cherries, drained

Place cranberry sauce in bowl and break up with fork. Add cherries and orange rind. Toss gently. Chill.

Delicious with chicken. Great for Rosh Hashana.

MARINATED MUSHROOMS WITH SCALLIONS

Yields: 2-4 servings

10 ounces assorted, exotic, fresh
    mushrooms

1 bunch green onions

DRESSING

2 tablespoons olive oil

2 tablespoons white vinegar

½ teaspoon salt

1 tablespoon sugar

Clean mushrooms. If tiny, leave whole. If regular size, cut into slices. Place in bowl. Chop green onions and add to mushrooms. In separate bowl, whisk together oil, white vinegar, salt and sugar. Taste for seasoning, adjust as necessary, then add to mushrooms and scallions. Allow to marinate at least 60 minutes. Stir and serve. Keeps at least a week in the refrigerator.

Green Beans, Corn and Pea Salad

Yields: 10-12 servings

1 (16-ounce) bag frozen French cut green beans, defrosted

1 (16-ounce) bag frozen shoe peg corn, defrosted

1 (16-ounce) bag frozen baby green peas, defrosted

1 red pepper, diced

½ red onion, finely diced

¼ cup sugar

⅓-½ cup white vinegar, to taste

¼ cup vegetable oil

1 teaspoon salt

½ teaspoon pepper

Combine all ingredients and allow to marinate.

Attractive, colorful buffet dish. Half a cup of blanched almonds or lightly salted cashews adds a nice crunch.

GREEK SALAD

Yields: 6-8 servings

SALAD

1 head romaine lettuce, torn into
    bite-size pieces
1 red onion, thinly sliced
1 (6-ounce) can pitted black olives

2 large tomatoes, quartered
1 cucumber, sliced
1 cup feta cheese, crumbled

DRESSING

6 tablespoons olive oil
1 teaspoon dried oregano
¼ teaspoon garlic powder

Juice of 1 lemon
Black pepper, to taste, freshly ground

Salad: In a large bowl, combine romaine lettuce, onion, olives, tomatoes, cucumbers and cheese.

Dressing: Whisk together olive oil, oregano, garlic powder, lemon juice and black pepper. Pour dressing over salad, toss and serve immediately.

Tarragon Chicken Salad

Yields: 6-8 servings

2 pounds chicken, cooked and diced
2 cups mayonnaise
3 tablespoons dried tarragon

1 cup white raisins, poached in water
    until plumped
Salt and pepper, to taste

Mix all ingredients together and season with salt and pepper to taste.

Chicken-Horseradish Salad

Yields: 6 servings

3 cups cooked chicken, chopped
½ cup green onions, chopped fine
2 celery stalks, chopped
½ cup pecans, chopped and toasted
⅔ cup light mayonnaise

2 to 3 tablespoons prepared
    horseradish
2 teaspoons fresh lemon juice
½ teaspoon lemon zest
¼ teaspoon salt
½ teaspoon pepper

Preheat oven to 350°. Toast pecans on baking sheet 8-10 minutes. Allow to cool, and then coarsely chop. Mix all ingredients in a large bowl and cover; chill at least 2 hours before serving.

A good use for leftover chicken.

SALAD WITH PINK DRESSING

Yields: 6 servings

SALAD
10 ounces Romaine lettuce
⅓ cup dried cranberries

⅓ cup pine nuts
1 cup fresh strawberries

DRESSING
1 medium purple onion, peeled and
    quartered
1 cup vinegar

2 teaspoons salt
½-¾ cup sugar
2 cups vegetable oil

Salad: Combine salad ingredients. Add enough dressing to coat salad. There will be some left over.

Dressing: Process onion, vinegar, salt and sugar in food processor or blender until smooth. Taste and correct sugar and salt, if necessary. Pour into quart size bottle, then add 2 cups oil and shake. (Do not put oil in when blending or it will get a milky look.) Dressing keeps at least a month in the refrigerator.

A kosher Chardonnay would make a nice accompaniment. Add dry cherries to accentuate fruit flavor and boost healthful properties.

CUCUMBER SALAD

Yields: 12-14 servings

3 large cucumbers, peeled and sliced
½ red onion, sliced thinly
1 cup water
1 cup white vinegar

1 cup sugar
Salt, to taste
1 small onion, sliced

Take sliced cucumbers and lightly salt them. Leave sitting for an hour or so. Mix water, vinegar and sugar together. Pour mixture over cucumbers. Add onions. Chill before serving.

Prepare Ahead of Time

BLACK BEAN SALAD

Yields: 6 servings

2 (15-ounce) cans black beans, drained and rinsed
1½ cups canned corn
1½ cups seeded tomatoes, chopped
¾ cup scallions, chopped

¼ cup olive oil
¼ cup lemon juice
2 teaspoons kosher salt
Pepper, to taste

Combine all ingredients. Chill.

For a Tex-Mex spin, add ¼ cup chopped fresh cilantro, ½ cup chopped green pepper, and 1 teaspoon chili powder.

MAJESTIC LAYERED SALAD

Yields: 8 servings

1 (10-ounce) package fresh spinach
2 cups fresh mushroom slices
1 (10-ounce) package frozen peas
¾-1 cup mayonnaise

½ teaspoon curry powder
Bacon flavored bits
½ teaspoon sugar

In a 2½-quart salad bowl, layer spinach, mushrooms, and peas. In a separate bowl, combine mayonnaise, sugar and curry powder. Spread over salad. Cover and refrigerate overnight. Top with bacon flavored bits before serving.

Add 1½ cups red onion rings, if desired.

Prepare Ahead of Time

CLAREMONT SALAD

Yields: 8-10 servings

SALAD
1 large cabbage, sliced thinly
1 medium onion, sliced
2 green peppers, diced

1 pound carrots, sliced
2 cans black olives, pitted

DRESSING
1½ cups sugar
2 cups white vinegar
¼ cup kosher salt

¼ cup vegetable oil
⅔ cup water

Salad: Combine all salad ingredients.

Dressing: Mix all ingredients and pour over salad. Best when prepared 3 or 4 days ahead. Will last several weeks. If desired, add a jar of chopped herring, drained.

Prepare Ahead of Time

A picnic meal, consisting of
bread dipped in olive oil, toasted wheat,
olives and fruit, was eaten by Ruth the Moabite,
and Boaz, her future husband.
(Ruth 2:14)

BRANDIED FRUIT SALAD

Yields: 12-15 servings

2 cantaloupes, peeled and diced
2 honeydews, peeled and diced
1 can pineapple
1 bag frozen strawberries
1 bag frozen raspberries

1 bag frozen blueberries
1 cup toasted slivered almonds
2 bags assorted dried fruit
1 cup apricot brandy or peach Schnapps

Combine all ingredients, chill overnight.

Prepare Ahead of Time

MARINATED BROCCOLI SALAD

Yields: 4-6 servings

SALAD
1 head broccoli, cut into bite-size pieces
¼ pound feta cheese
½ pint cherry tomatoes, halved

1 small package slivered almonds, toasted
½ small bag radishes, sliced and roasted

DRESSING
½ cup olive oil
3 tablespoons white or red wine vinegar

1 garlic clove, chopped
½-1 teaspoon salt
Pepper, to taste

Salad: Mix together all ingredients.

Dressing: Mix all ingredients and pour over salad ingredients. Marinate 6 hours before serving. Toss frequently.

A low-carb favorite, colorful and heart healthy.

Prepare Ahead of Time

TABBOULEH

Yields: 6-8 servings

1 cup bulgur (cracked wheat)
½ cup minced green onions
1 cup finely chopped parsley
4 medium tomatoes, peeled, seeded
    and chopped
⅓ cup lemon juice

Salt and pepper, to taste
⅓ cup olive oil
Romaine lettuce
Pita bread, cut into triangles
Lemon slices to garnish

Place bulgur in bowl with cold water to cover. Soak 20 minutes. Drain well and squeeze out water. Place drained bulgur in a large bowl. Add rest of ingredients, except lettuce and lemon. Allow to marinate 30 minutes. Stir well.

Spoon mixture onto large platter and surround with lettuce leaves or pita bread triangles to be used as scoops. Garnish with lemon slices.

Optional ingredient — ¼ cup fresh chopped mint leaves.

The most widespread bread among the Sephardi Jewish people is the Arab flatbread with a pocket — pita.

FATOOSH

Yields: 4-6 servings

2 large pita breads
8 leaves romaine lettuce, torn into
    bite-size pieces
2 green onions, chopped
1 cucumber, chopped
3 tomatoes, cut into wedges
¼ cup chopped fresh parsley

1 garlic clove, peeled and chopped
2 tablespoons sumac powder
¼ cup lemon juice
¼ cup olive oil
1 teaspoon salt
¼ teaspoon ground black pepper
¼ cup chopped fresh mint leaves

Preheat oven to 350°. Toast pitas 5-10 minutes until crisp. Remove from heat and break into bite-size pieces, set aside. In a large bowl, toss together romaine lettuce, green onions, cucumber and tomatoes. In a small bowl, mix remaining ingredients. Pour over the vegetable mixture. Add pita pieces and toss before serving.

Sumac powder is a Middle Eastern spice with a fruity yet sour flavor. It is available at Middle Eastern markets or from several websites. A substitute is sweet paprika.

Chef's Pick

CURRIED RICE SALAD

Yields: 8-10 servings

1½ cups cooked rice
¼ cup onion, minced
1 tablespoon vinegar
½ cup mayonnaise
2 tablespoons salad oil
¾ teaspoon curry powder
1½ teaspoons salt

⅓ cup green pepper, minced
1 cup celery, chopped
2 cups frozen green peas, defrosted
Toasted almonds, chopped
Parsley, optional
Pimento, optional

Mix together rice and onion. In a separate bowl, whisk together vinegar, mayonnaise, oil, curry powder and salt. Pour dressing over rice mixture and refrigerate 3 hours or overnight. Prior to serving, add green pepper, celery and peas. Sprinkle with almonds and parsley or pimento if desired.

Prepare Ahead of Time

COLESLAW SOUFFLÉ SALAD

Yields: 4 servings

1 package lemon gelatin
1 cup hot water
½ cup mayonnaise
½ cup cold water
2 tablespoons vinegar
¼ teaspoon salt

1½ cups grated cabbage
½ cup radish slices
½ cup diced celery
3 tablespoons diced green pepper
1 tablespoon diced onion

Dissolve gelatin in hot water. Blend in mayonnaise, cold water, vinegar and salt. Chill until practically set. Beat until fluffy. Add remaining ingredients. Pour into 1 quart mold and chill until solid.

CRANBERRY SALAD MOLD

Yields: 6-8 servings

1 (3-ounce) package cherry gelatin
1 cup hot water
½ teaspoon salt
1 pound cranberries, ground

1 orange
1 small can crushed pineapple
1 cup sugar
¾ cup nuts, chopped coarsely

Dissolve gelatin in hot water. Add salt and set aside to cool. In food processor, grind ½ orange with rind. Squeeze juice from other half and set aside. Mix crushed pineapple with sugar. Add nuts. Mix all ingredients together, pour into mold. Refrigerate in mold until set, about 4 hours. Unmold and garnish with fresh fruit or mint sprigs.

ASIAN CRUNCH SALAD

Yields: 8 servings

1 cup broccoli florets
1 cup cauliflower
1 cup cherry or grape tomatoes
½ cup fresh snow peas
2 green onions, thinly sliced
½ cup sliced water chestnuts, drained
4½ teaspoons reduced-sodium soy
    sauce

1 tablespoon cider vinegar
1 tablespoon sesame oil
¾ teaspoon sugar
½ teaspoon sesame seeds, toasted
½ teaspoon olive oil
Dash of pepper

Cut broccoli and cauliflower into bite-size pieces, then steam 2-3 minutes until fork-tender but not soft.

In a large bowl, combine broccoli, cauliflower, tomatoes, snow peas and onions. Stir in water chestnuts. In a small bowl, whisk together remainder of ingredients. Pour over vegetable mixture; stir to coat. Cover and refrigerate until chilled.

This is a colorful addition to any meal or a terrific low-cal crunchy snack. Recipe can easily be doubled.

In order to ensure a sufficient quantity of etrogim, the Jews were the ones who planted citrus orchards around the Mediterranean, founding the citrus market.

TROPICAL SALAD WITH ORANGE DRESSING

Yields: 4 servings

SALAD
1 Granny Smith apple, peeled and diced
Juice of 1 lime
1 cup pineapple, diced
½ cup seedless red grapes, halved

1 celery stalk, diced
¼ cup almonds, coarsely chopped
Salt and pepper, to taste

DRESSING
2 cups fresh orange juice
½ cup nonfat plain yogurt

½ cup light mayonnaise
Zest of ½ orange

Salad: Toss apple and lime juice. Add remaining ingredients. Fold in dressing. Season with salt and pepper.

Dressing: Bring orange juice to a boil. Lower heat, cook until juice is reduced to 3 or 4 tablespoons of very thick syrup, about 25-30 minutes. Combine yogurt and mayonnaise in a bowl with 2 tablespoons of the syrup and the zest. Cover and refrigerate until needed.

SAVORY SPINACH SALAD

Yields: 4 servings

SALAD
1 pound fresh baby spinach, stemmed, rinsed and dried

1 small red onion, thinly sliced and separated into rings

1 (8-ounce) smoked trout, skinned and cut into 1-inch pieces

4 ounces mild bleu cheese, coarsely crumbled

DRESSING
1 cup dry white wine

¼ cup olive oil

1 tablespoon balsamic vinegar

¾ teaspoon salt

¼ teaspoon freshly ground pepper

¼ cup shelled hazelnuts, toasted and coarsely chopped

Salad: In a large bowl, combine spinach, onion rings and trout. Cover and refrigerate. Pour dressing over salad and toss. Divide evenly among four plates. Top each serving with crumbled bleu cheese.

Dressing: In a small saucepan, boil the wine until reduced to 2 tablespoons. Whisk in oil, vinegar, salt and pepper. Add nuts and warm the mixture over medium heat.

Substitute other smoked fish if trout not available.

ORZO SALAD WITH FETA

Yields: 10-15 servings

SALAD

12 ounces orzo
1 tablespoon olive oil
1½ cups feta cheese, crumbled
1 cup red bell pepper, chopped

1 cup yellow bell pepper, chopped
¾ cup black olives, pitted
4 green onions, chopped
2 tablespoons capers, drained

DRESSING

3 tablespoons fresh lemon juice
1 tablespoon white wine vinegar
1 tablespoon garlic, minced
1 teaspoon Dijon mustard

1 teaspoon ground cumin, optional
½ cup olive oil
3 tablespoons pine nuts, toasted

Salad: Cook orzo in a large pot of boiling, salted water until tender but still firm to bite. Drain, rinse with cold water, and drain well. Transfer to a large bowl and toss with 2 tablespoons olive oil. Add feta cheese, peppers, olives, onions and capers. Toss with dressing. Garnish salad with pine nuts.

Dressing: Combine lemon juice, vinegar, garlic, mustard and cumin in a small bowl. Gradually whisk in remaining ½ cup olive oil. Season dressing to taste with salt and pepper. Can be prepared 6 hours ahead. Cover and refrigerate.

The Caesar salad was
created in Tijuana, Mexico, in a hotel
restaurant owned by Cesar and
Alex Cardini, on the 4th of
July, 1924.

CAESAR SALAD

Yields: 6-8 servings

Salt
1 clove garlic, peeled
1 teaspoon dry mustard
1 tablespoon lemon juice
Few drops Worcestershire sauce
Tabasco, to taste
3 tablespoons olive oil

3 bunches romaine lettuce, torn into
  bite-size pieces
2 tablespoons grated Parmesan
  cheese
1 (20-ounce) can anchovies, drained,
  if desired
½ cup croutons

Sprinkle bottom of wooden salad bowl with salt and rub in the garlic. Add mustard, lemon juice, Worcestershire sauce and Tabasco. Stir until salt dissolves. Add olive oil, stirring until blended. Add romaine to salad bowl, sprinkle with Parmesan cheese and anchovies, if desired. Sprinkle with croutons and gently mix. Serve immediately.

SPANISH CHICKEN SALAD

Yields: 4 servings

1 cup frozen peas
2 cups water
1 cup regular long grain rice
1 teaspoon chicken flavor bouillon
¼ teaspoon saffron threads
1 teaspoon salt
2 whole chicken breasts
3 tablespoons salad oil

¼ teaspoon pepper
¾ teaspoon fresh thyme or ¼ teaspoon dried thyme leaves
½ (7-ounce) jar roasted, sweet red peppers, drained and cut into ¼-inch thick strips
¼ pound salami, cut into bite-size pieces, optional

About 1 hour before serving or early in day, place frozen peas in a small bowl. Cover with boiling water and let stand to "cook" peas. In 2-quart saucepan over high heat, heat 2 cups water to boiling. Stir in rice, bouillon, saffron and 1 teaspoon salt. Bring back to a boil. Reduce heat to low, cover and simmer 20 minutes or until rice is tender and all liquid absorbed. Remove rice to a large bowl and set aside. Cut chicken into ⅛-inch thick strips. In 3-quart saucepan heat salad oil over high heat, cook chicken, pepper and 1½ teaspoons salt stirring quickly and constantly, just until chicken loses its pink color and is tender. Remove from heat. Stir in thyme. Add chicken with juices to rice. Drain peas. Add peas, roasted peppers and salami to chicken mixture. Toss lightly.

If not serving right away, cover and refrigerate to serve well-chilled.

Spicy Eggplant Salad

Yields: 4-6 servings

1 medium to large eggplant
¼ pound mushrooms, thinly sliced
1 tablespoon olive oil
10 green cocktail olives, with pimentos
½ green bell pepper
Salt, to taste

1 small onion
1 garlic clove
2 tablespoons chopped fresh parsley
   or cilantro
¼ teaspoon red chili powder
Pepper, to taste

Prick eggplant and grill directly over a burner on top of stove until skin is charred and flesh soft, or in oven at 400° for 1 hour until soft throughout. Allow to cool. Peel, remove those seeds that can easily be removed, chop. Sauté mushrooms in olive oil until they are just beginning to turn brown. Dice or mince mushrooms, olives, green pepper and onion. Mince garlic. Combine all ingredients. Mix rapidly, so the eggplant does not become a paste.

This can be served as part of a salad plate or as a salsa. Except for the onion, it will keep in the refrigerator several days. If it is not to be eaten at once, add onion only just before serving.

Proportions are flexible, depending on taste. Hotter peppers, such as Poblano or Anaheim, can be substituted for the green bell pepper. The red chili powder can be increased or omitted. Garlic may be omitted or increased to 2 cloves. A teaspoon or two of cold water or vinegar may be added.

CORN-BARLEY SALAD

Yields: 6-8 servings

SALAD

1½ cups water
1½ cups vegetable broth
¾ cup barley, checked and rinsed
2 cups frozen corn, thawed

1 cup scallions, thinly sliced
¼ cup pimentos, chopped
½ cup chopped fresh cilantro and/or
    parsley

DRESSING

¼ cup apple cider vinegar
2 cloves garlic, peeled
½ teaspoon ground cumin
½ teaspoon mild chili powder

2 teaspoons sugar
½ teaspoon salt
½ teaspoon ground black pepper
½ cup canola oil

Salad: Bring water and broth to a boil in a 2-quart saucepan. Add barley, stir, and lower heat. Cover and simmer 30- 35 minutes until al dente. Drain, rinse with cold water. Place barley in a bowl to cool, then add corn, scallions and pimentos. Mix well.

Dressing: Purée vinegar and garlic in a blender or food processor. Add cumin, chili powder, sugar, salt and pepper. As the mixture combines, pour oil in a slow, steady stream and blend several seconds more. Taste dressing and adjust seasonings to taste. Toss salad with dressing, cilantro and/or parsley. Cover, refrigerate for several hours before serving.

A marvelous change from your ordinary salads! You can substitute jarred roasted peppers for pimentos.

Chef's Choice

Beet Salad with Horseradish and Fried Capers

Yields: 4 servings

1½ pounds small beets, trimmed and scrubbed

Olive oil for baking and frying

2 tablespoons salt-packed or brined capers

1 clove garlic, crushed

Sea salt, to taste

DRESSING

1 tablespoon Dijon mustard

1½ tablespoons horseradish

¼ cup white wine vinegar

¼ cup olive oil

1 tablespoon sour cream

Preheat oven to 350°. Place beets on one end of a foil sheet, drizzle with small amount of olive oil, fold over and crimp edges of foil. Place on baking sheet and roast until beets are tender, 45-60 minutes. (Test by poking a fork through foil into the beet.) Remove from oven. While beets are still warm, peel and slice them into wedges and place in a bowl. Soak salt-packed capers 10 minutes; drain, rinse, then pat dry. (If using brined capers, drain and pat dry.) Fry capers in small amount of hot olive oil until they fluff and begin to brown on edges, 30-60 seconds. Drain on paper towels. In a small bowl, whisk together mustard, horseradish and vinegar. Whisk in ¼ cup olive oil, followed by sour cream. Pour half the dressing over beets, mix. Taste, adding more dressing or salt if needed. Rub a platter with crushed garlic, then spoon on beets and sprinkle with fried capers and sea salt.

For a more intense flavor, substitute balsamic vinegar for white wine vinegar.

BASIC VINAIGRETTE

Yields: ¾ cup

½ cup extra virgin olive oil
¼ cup red wine vinegar
1 tablespoon onion, finely chopped

½ teaspoon salt
1 teaspoon fresh basil, finely chopped
¼ teaspoon crushed black pepper

Combine all ingredients and mix well with a fork or in a shaker bottle.

CLASSIC FRENCH DRESSING

Yields: 1½ cups

1 cup extra light olive oil
¼ cup white wine vinegar
¼ cup lemon juice

½ teaspoon salt
½ teaspoon dry mustard
½ teaspoon paprika

Shake all ingredients in a tightly covered container.

To make Red French Dressing: *Mix ½ cup Classic French Dressing with ½ cup ketchup.*

CAESAR SALAD DRESSING

Yields: 1½ cups

3 finely chopped garlic cloves
2 eggs
1 tablespoon lemon juice

½ teaspoon salt
½ teaspoon pepper
1 cup oil

Combine ingredients except oil in food processor. While processing, slowly add oil.

Pour over romaine lettuce and add croutons.

CREAMY HONEY DIJON MUSTARD DRESSING

Yields: 1½ cups

1 cup mayonnaise
3 tablespoons honey

2 tablespoons plus 1 teaspoon vinegar
2 teaspoons Dijon mustard

Combine all ingredients.

Serve over leaf lettuce, grapes, oranges, almonds, onions, etc.

Feta Cheese Dressing

Yields: 1½ cups

1 cup olive oil
¼ cup lemon juice
Salt and pepper, to taste

2 garlic cloves, crushed
Oregano, to taste
½ pound feta cheese, crumbled

Combine oil and lemon juice. Add salt, pepper, garlic and oregano. Mix well. Crumble feta cheese into mixture and refrigerate overnight. Serve at room temperature.

Sesame Orange Dressing

Yields: 2 cups

1 cup sour cream
1 cup mayonnaise
¼ cup orange juice concentrate,
    undiluted

2 tablespoons toasted sesame oil
1½ tablespoons soy sauce
½ tablespoon grated fresh ginger
Pinch cayenne pepper

Combine all ingredients in mixing bowl and thoroughly stir together. For thinner dressing, add water 1 teaspoon at a time until desired consistency is reached.

GARLIC SALAD DRESSING

Yields: 1 cup

1-2 large garlic cloves, minced
⅔ cup olive or other vegetable oil
   (or combination)
⅓ cup wine vinegar or tarragon vinegar
½ teaspoon salt

½ teaspoon freshly ground pepper
½ teaspoon dry mustard
1 teaspoon Worcestershire sauce
¼ cup freshly grated Parmesan cheese

Combine all ingredients in a glass jar and shake well. Make dressing one day before serving.

Prepare ahead of time

RUSSIAN DRESSING

Yields: 1½ cups

1 cup mayonnaise
2 tablespoons sweet pickle relish
¼ cup ketchup

1 teaspoon chopped onion
½ teaspoon paprika
1 teaspoon prepared horseradish

Combine all ingredients and mix well.

Salads

Thomas Jefferson
was the country's first well-known
gourmet. He had the foresight to import the first
macaroni, Parmesan cheese, figs, raisins, mustard,
anchovies and vanilla to the United States.

Sweet and Sour Salad Dressing

Yields: 1¾ cups

1 cup vegetable oil
½ cup cider vinegar
1 clove garlic, minced

2 teaspoons salt
1 teaspoon cracked pepper
3 tablespoons sugar

Combine all ingredients and shake well. Chill.

Essential Vinaigrette

Yields: 2 cups

6 tablespoons cider vinegar
3 tablespoons fresh lemon juice
4 teaspoons Dijon mustard

1 teaspoon salt
¼ teaspoon pepper
1½ cups safflower oil

Whisk together vinegar, lemon juice, mustard, salt, and pepper in a stainless steel bowl. Add oil in slow stream while whisking.

Meat

*After the designated hours,
the manna melted and formed brooks
which were frequented by deer and rams.
These animals were hunted and eaten
by the nations who found that the meat
possessed a marvelous and extraordinary
flavor like that of the manna.*

(Midrash Tanchuma, Parshas Beshalach)

Just a Reminder...
green = pareve   red = meat   blue = dairy

FAIL-PROOF RIB ROAST

Yields: 6-8 servings

Rib roast (3-7 ribs)
Flour for dusting

Kosher salt, to taste
Pepper, to taste

Preheat oven to 500°. Dust entire roast in flour, salt and pepper. Put roast into oven and cook for exactly 5 minutes per pound of meat. Turn oven off and leave for 2 hours. Do not open oven! Remove roast and let stand 5 minutes before carving.

Chef's Choice

CHILI

Yields: 4-6 servings

1 pound ground beef or turkey,
    browned
1 large onion, diced
2 (1-pound) cans spicy chili beans
1 (6-ounce) can tomato paste
2 cups water

1 teaspoon salt
2 teaspoons chili powder
1 teaspoon cumin
1 tablespoon parsley
½ teaspoon pepper

Combine all ingredients in a Dutch oven over medium-high heat and bring to a boil. Lower heat and simmer at least 45 minutes.

In the old days, the cholent pot was hermetically sealed with a flour and water paste, and cooked in the town baker's oven.

BARLEY-LESS CHOLENT

Yields: 8-10 servings

1½ pounds stew chuck
Bones, optional
4-5 medium potatoes, peeled and
    quartered
1 medium onion, peeled and quartered
1½ cups assorted beans
    (kidney, navy, black-eye)
⅓ cup ketchup

¼ cup cream of wheat, optional
½ cup rice, optional
2-3 tablespoons cornstarch, optional
Salt, to taste
Pepper, to taste
Garlic powder, to taste
Water to fill pot

Preheat crockpot on medium-high. Assemble all ingredients in the pot. Cover with water. Cook overnight.

All of the proportions are approximate and you might want to experiment with your crockpot temperature settings. Using a lot of bones will greatly improve the cholent. Beans can be presoaked the night before.

Prepare Ahead of Time

CHOLENT

Yields: 10-12 servings

1 or 2 pounds stew meat
5 medium potatoes, peeled and cut into
  chunks
1 large onion, cut into chunks
1 cup dry navy beans, soaked at least
  3 hours
1 cup barley

⅛ cup molasses
⅛ cup honey
¼ cup ketchup
3 tablespoons beef broth
Salt and pepper, to taste
Water

Preheat crockpot to low. Place meat, potatoes, onion, navy beans, and barley in pot. Add remaining ingredients. Add water until contents are barely covered. Cook overnight until cholent contents are tender and ready to serve.

Enjoy this cholent with its slight barbecue flavor.

The word "cholent" is believed to have come from a medieval French contraction of chauld (hot) and lent (slow).

MEAT CHOLENT

Yields: 10-12 servings

2 cups dried lima beans
3 pounds stew meat
3 onions, diced
3 tablespoons vegetable oil
2 teaspoons salt

Black pepper, to taste
¼ teaspoon ground ginger
1 cup pearl barley
2 tablespoons flour
Paprika, to taste

Cover beans with water and soak overnight. Drain. Using a heavy saucepan or Dutch oven, brown meat and onions in oil. Sprinkle with salt, pepper and ginger. Add beans and barley and sprinkle with flour and paprika. Add enough boiling water to cover one inch above mixture. Cover tightly. Cholent may be baked 24 hours at 250°. For quicker cooking, bake at 350°, 4-5 hours.

Prepare Ahead of Time

Short Ribs "Aloha"

Yields: 4-6 servings

3 pounds short ribs
Salt and pepper, to taste
½ cup finely chopped onions
¼ cup chopped green pepper
2 (8-ounce) cans tomato sauce

1 tablespoon Worcestershire sauce
⅓ cup vinegar
2½ cups pineapple
¼ cup brown sugar
½ teaspoon dry mustard

Preheat oven to 350°. Sprinkle salt and pepper on short ribs. Place in shallow roasting pan and bake 60 minutes. Pour off excess fat. While ribs are roasting, mix remaining ingredients and let stand to blend flavors. Pour over ribs. Bake 50-60 minutes longer, basting frequently to glaze ribs.

Glazed Corned Beef

Yields: 8 servings

4-5 pounds corned beef
2 tablespoons margarine
5 tablespoons ketchup

1 tablespoon mustard
3 tablespoons white vinegar
⅓ cup brown sugar

Place corned beef in large pot and cover with cold water. Bring to boil and simmer until tender, about 3-4 hours. Drain and chill in refrigerator. Preheat oven to 350°. Slice chilled beef and place in large casserole. Combine margarine, ketchup, mustard, vinegar and sugar in a saucepan. Bring to a boil. Pour over meat. Bake uncovered 30 minutes or until brown. Baste occasionally.

There are probably as many different stuffed cabbage recipes as there are towns in Central and Eastern Europe, where this dish originated.

"UNSTUFFED" CABBAGE AND MEATBALLS

Yields: 8-10 servings

MEAT MIXTURE

2 pounds chopped beef
1 egg, beaten
1 onion, grated

¾ cup seasoned bread crumbs or ¼ cup matzo meal
Salt, pepper, garlic, to taste

SAUCE

1 can whole cranberry sauce
1 (16-ounce) can tomato sauce
2 tablespoons cider vinegar

1 teaspoon each onion powder and garlic powder
1 teaspoon sugar
Salt and pepper, to taste

CABBAGE MIXTURE

2 pounds cabbage (packages of already grated cabbage can be used)

3 carrots, grated

Preheat oven to 350°.

Meat Mixture: Combine all ingredients. Form into small balls. Bake 10 minutes.

Sauce: Mix all ingredients together in a pan. Bring to a boil; add meatballs. Reduce heat to simmer; partially cover and continue cooking about 1 hour.

Cabbage Mixture: Place cabbage mixture on the bottom of a roasting pan. Pour sauce and meatballs on top of cabbage. Cover and bake about 45 minutes.

This is a delicious and much easier way to make "stuffed" cabbage, while retaining the traditional flavor.

MARINATED FLANK STEAK

Yields: 6-8 servings

1 (2-pound) flank steak, scored
1½ cups olive oil
¾ cup soy sauce
½ cup wine vinegar
½ cup fresh lemon juice

¼ cup Worcestershire sauce
2 tablespoons Dijon mustard
1 tablespoon ground pepper
1 large sprig parsley
2 garlic cloves, crushed

Place steak in flat dish or bowl. Combine remaining ingredients in blender and whirl briefly. Pour over meat. Cover and refrigerate 12-24 hours, turning occasionally with tongs.

Before cooking, prepare barbecue or preheat broiler. Remove meat from marinade. Barbecue or broil steak until well browned on outside and still pink within. Cut meat into thin slices across the grain.

Meat

STOVE-TOP BARBECUE BRISKET

Yields: 6-8 servings

1 (3-pound) brisket, cut in chunks
1½ cups ketchup
3 large onions, chopped
6 tablespoons sugar

6 tablespoons white vinegar
6 teaspoons yellow mustard
3 tablespoons Worcestershire sauce
Hot sauce, to taste

In a pan, combine ketchup, onion, sugar, vinegar, mustard and Worcestershire into a sauce. Cook brisket in sauce on stove-top, medium heat, covered, until tender, about 2 hours. Shred brisket and put back in sauce. Add hot sauce to taste. Serve on party rolls.

SWEET AND SOUR BRISKET

Yields: 8 servings

4 pounds beef brisket
½ teaspoon salt
¼ teaspoon pepper
½ teaspoon garlic powder
3 large onions, sliced

10 ounces lemon-lime carbonated
    beverage
1 cup ketchup
½ cup brown sugar
1 teaspoon ginger
½ cup raisins

Season brisket with salt, pepper and garlic powder. Sear in large Dutch oven. Add onions. Pour lemon-lime beverage over meat and onions, cover and cook 3 hours over medium-low heat. Cool. Remove meat from pot. Add ketchup, brown sugar, ginger and raisins to pan drippings. Slice meat and return to sauce. Cook 30 minutes longer over low heat.

During the time
of the First Temple Period, meat
was enjoyed only by the privileged rich.
Ordinary people only ate meat on
special occasions and holidays.

BEER BRISKET

Yields: 8 servings

3-4 pounds beef brisket
1 (12-ounce) can beer

1 (12-ounce) bottle chili sauce
1 package dry onion soup mix

Preheat oven to 325°. Mix together beer, chili sauce and onion soup. Pour over brisket in roasting pan. Cover tightly and bake 3 hours or until tender. Remove from oven. Let cool. Slice brisket against the grain. Put slices back in sauce and re-heat until warm.

Quick n Easy

VEAL STROGANOFF

Yields: 4-6 servings

1½-2 pounds veal stew
1 large egg, beaten
6-8 tablespoons bread crumbs
1 tablespoon oil

1 (5¾-ounce) can mushroom steak
   sauce
1 cup pareve sour cream

Preheat oven to 350°. Dip veal in egg, then coat with bread crumbs. Fry in oil until lightly browned. Remove to bottom of baking dish. Mix steak sauce and sour cream together. Pour over veal. Cover and bake 1 hour. Serve over rice.

VEAL CHOPS

Yields: 4 servings

MARINADE
2 tablespoons cumin   1 teaspoon salt
½ tablespoon garlic powder   ½ teaspoon pepper

CHOPS
4 veal chops   1½ large onions cut into rings
3 tablespoons oil

Mix together marinade ingredients. Rub veal chops with marinade and let marinate at least 1 hour. Make sure to divide seasoning so both sides of chops are marinated with ingredients equally.

Heat 2 tablespoons oil in a pan over medium heat. Sauté chops on each side 4-5 minutes. Do not let burn. Add a little more oil if necessary. Set aside in warm oven, or cover so they don't cool too much.

Add remaining oil to pan in which chops were cooked. Place onion rings in pan and sauté about 5 minutes until light brown.

Top veal chops with onions and serve.

BEEF AND ONION STIR FRY

Yields: 8-10 servings

2 pounds sirloin steak, ¼-inch thick or
    flank, cut into thin slices
5 tablespoons peanut oil
4 cups sliced onions
4 tablespoons sherry

4 tablespoons soy sauce
1 teaspoon sugar
1 tablespoon cornstarch
Fresh sliced mushrooms, optional

Preheat 2½ tablespoons peanut oil in a skillet or a wok. Sauté onions 3 minutes. Add 2 tablespoons sherry, 2 tablespoons soy sauce, ½ teaspoon sugar. Cook 10 seconds, remove from pan. Toss meat with cornstarch, 2 tablespoons sherry, 2 tablespoons soy sauce and ½ teaspoon sugar. Heat 2½ tablespoons peanut oil and brown meat. Return onions to pan and add mushrooms, if desired. Cook 2 minutes. Serve over rice.

SIMPLY-DONE MEATLOAF

Yields: 8 servings

1 pound chopped beef
1 slice soft bread, broken into small
    pieces
1 egg
1 large can tomato sauce
1 small onion, chopped

1 green pepper cut in half
    (chop half and slice half)
Salt and pepper, to taste
2 heaping teaspoons brown sugar
1 teaspoon apple cider or white vinegar
2 tablespoons mustard

Preheat oven to 450°. Mix beef, bread, egg, ½ can tomato sauce, onion and chopped green pepper. Salt and pepper to taste. Form into loaf, cover and bake 20 minutes. Remove from oven and drain fat. Reduce temperature to 350°. In a separate pan, combine the other half of tomato sauce with brown sugar, vinegar and mustard. Bring slowly to a boil, stirring constantly. Remove from heat; pour over meatloaf. Place green pepper strips on top. Bake 40 minutes uncovered.

JAMBALAYA

Yields: 4-6 servings

¾ cup uncooked rice
3 tablespoons vegetable oil
1 clove garlic, diced
2 green peppers, chopped
1 cup chopped onion
1 pound ground beef
¼ teaspoon Worcestershire sauce

1 tablespoon chopped parsley
¼ teaspoon paprika
1 bay leaf
1 (28-ounce) can whole tomatoes
1 teaspoon chili powder
1½ teaspoons salt
½ teaspoon black pepper

Cook rice according to package instructions. Place oil in heavy skillet and sauté garlic. Add peppers and onions and sauté until soft. Push to one side of pan and brown meat. Add remaining ingredients. Cover and simmer 20 minutes.

Adding chicken pieces and kosher sausage will make this recipe more authentic.

Chef's Choice

CHINESE POT ROAST

Yields: 12 servings

1 tablespoon minced garlic
1 teaspoon fresh, grated ginger
1 teaspoon salt
½ teaspoon Chinese five-spice powder
1 (5-pound) chuck roast
⅓ cup soy sauce
¼ cup brown sugar
¼ cup cooking sherry
2 tablespoons vegetable oil

1½ cups water
3 potatoes, peeled and cubed
3 carrots, cut into 2-inch pieces
1 stalk celery, cut into 2-inch pieces
1 onion, cut into wedges
3 tablespoons cornstarch
¼ cup cold water
2 green onions, chopped

Combine garlic, ginger, salt and five-spice powder. Rub spice mixture over surface of roast. Place roast in ungreased 13 x 9 x 2-inch dish. Combine soy sauce, brown sugar and sherry. Pour marinade over roast. Cover, marinate in refrigerator 30 minutes, turning once.

Remove roast from marinade, reserving liquid. Brown roast in oil in large Dutch oven. Pour reserved marinade and 1½ cups water over roast. Bring to a boil; cover, reduce heat; simmer 2 hours. Add vegetables. Cook additional 30 minutes until vegetables are tender. Remove roast and vegetables to a serving platter. Cover to keep warm.

Heat reserved pan juices until boiling. Combine cornstarch and cold water, stirring until smooth. Add cornstarch mixture and green onions to pan juices. Cook over medium heat, stirring constantly, until thickened. Serve roast with warm sauce.

Meat

STUFFED CABBAGE FOR A CROWD

Yields: 4-5 servings per pound of meat mixture

MEAT MIXTURE

5 pounds ground chuck
5 eggs
½ large onion, grated
1 cup bread crumbs
  (or matzo meal for Passover)

Salt, pepper, garlic powder, to taste
½ cup water
3 large heads of cabbage, steamed

SAUCE

2 (28-ounce) cans whole plum
  tomatoes, crushed
½ large onion, grated

1 box dark brown sugar
1 cup lemon juice

Preheat oven to 350°.

Meat Mixture: Combine ground chuck, eggs, grated onion, bread crumbs and seasonings. Add enough bread crumbs and water until the mixture holds together like hamburger patties. Separate cabbage leaves and add enough meat to roll up until all meat and cabbage are used. Place in roasting pan. Leftover cabbage can be cut up and laid on top of rolls.

Sauce: Combine all ingredients and pour over cabbage rolls. Cover and bake 2 hours. Uncover and continue to cook 1 hour. Refrigerate overnight. Skim off any fat. For stronger taste, add an additional 1 cup dark brown sugar and ½ cup fresh lemon juice. Reheat and serve.

Like Bubbe made!

Prepare Ahead of Time

LAMB RAGOÛT

Yields: 6 servings

2 pounds boneless shoulder lamb
2 tablespoons vegetable oil
3¼ cups water
3 tablespoons tomato paste
3 teaspoons dry instant chicken
    bouillon
1 teaspoon salt
¼ teaspoon pepper

3 medium potatoes, quartered
6 small onions, quartered
3 medium carrots, cut into
    1½-inch pieces
3 small turnips, quartered
1 (10-ounce) package frozen peas
2 tablespoons all-purpose flour

Preheat Dutch oven to medium-high heat. Trim excess fat from lamb and cut lamb into 1-inch cubes. Cook in oil until brown, about 20 minutes; drain. Add 3 cups water, tomato paste, bouillon, salt and pepper. Heat to boiling, then reduce heat. Cover and simmer until lamb is almost tender, about 45 minutes.

Stir in potatoes, onions, carrots and turnips. Cover and simmer until vegetables are almost tender, about 30 minutes. Stir in peas. Cover and simmer until vegetables are tender, about 10 minutes more.

Shake flour with ¼ cup water in tightly covered container; gradually stir into ragoût. Heat to boiling, stirring constantly. Boil and stir 1 minute.

For beef ragoût, use 2 pounds beef (boneless chuck, tip or round) and beef bouillon. Increase first simmering time to about 1 hour.

TENDER BISON ROAST

Yields: 6-8 servings

1 bison roast, any flat cut
1 cup pasta sauce
1 cup dry or semi-dry red wine

Garlic, to taste
Pepper, to taste
Bed of vegetables, optional

Preheat oven to 350°. Rinse bison and place in baking dish that is just a little bigger than the roast. Combine pasta sauce with wine and pour over roast. Sprinkle liberally with garlic and pepper to taste. Cover with parchment paper and heavy-duty aluminum foil, seal edges. Bake 30 minutes and then reduce heat to 250° for 45 minutes per pound.

If a bed of vegetables is desired, chop 2 onions, 2-3 potatoes, 4 stalks of celery and 2-3 carrots. Place in pan before bison. If placing bison on vegetables, bake at 350° for 30 minutes per pound for the first 4 pounds and 20 minutes per pound for every pound after that.

Allow bison to cool slightly before cutting.

The parchment paper provides a layer of protection between the acidic pasta sauce and the foil so that the foil will not flake off on the meat.

If bison not available locally, try www.kosherbison.com.

BRISKET OF BEEF

Yields 8-10 servings

5½ pounds beef brisket, trimmed of fat
1½ teaspoons salt
¼ teaspoon ground pepper
3 tablespoons olive oil
2 whole garlic cloves, minced
3 large onions, thinly sliced

2 cups dry red wine
5 medium carrots, peeled and cut
   into 2-inch pieces
2 celery stalks, diced
1 (28-ounce) can plum tomatoes
   with juice

Preheat oven to 325°. Season both sides of beef well with salt and pepper. Heat 2 tablespoons olive oil in a heavy casserole over medium-high heat. Add brisket and brown very well, about 4 or 5 minutes each side. Transfer to a plate and set aside. Reduce heat to medium low. Add remaining olive oil, garlic and onions. Cook, stirring frequently, until quite brown and very soft, about 25 minutes. Add red wine, raise heat to high and bring to a boil. Cook about 2 minutes, scraping up the brown bits on the bottom of the pot. Add carrots, celery and tomatoes and stir well to combine. Return brisket to the pot, spooning some of the liquid and vegetables over it. Cover and transfer to oven. Bake 3 hours or until very tender, carefully turning meat after 1½ hours.

Let cool slightly and remove brisket, being careful not to shred. Transfer the sauce and vegetables from the pot to a food processor and process until very smooth. Adjust seasoning with salt and pepper if necessary. If serving right away, return sauce to the pot, slice meat across the grain into ¼-inch thick slices and place in sauce. Warm over medium-low heat for about 5 minutes.

ZINFANDEL-BRAISED BRISKET DINNER

Yields: 8 servings

2 cups Zinfandel or other fruity dry red wine

½ cup fat-free, low-sodium chicken broth

¼ cup tomato paste

1 (2½-pound) beef brisket, trimmed of fat

2 teaspoons salt

Cooking spray

4 medium sweet onions, chopped

2 tablespoons sugar

1¼ teaspoons dried thyme

6 garlic cloves, thinly sliced

2 carrots, peeled and cut into ½-inch slices

2 celery stalks, cut into ½-inch slices

1½ pounds small red potatoes, cut into quarters

1½ teaspoons extra virgin olive oil

½ teaspoon ground black pepper

1 teaspoon dried oregano

¼ teaspoon ground red pepper

Chopped fresh parsley

Combine wine, chicken broth and tomato paste and stir with a whisk. Heat large Dutch oven over medium-high heat. Sprinkle beef with ¾ teaspoon salt and ¼ teaspoon black pepper. Coat pan with cooking spray. Add beef to pan; cook 8 minutes, browning on all sides. Remove beef from pan, cover and set aside. Add ½ teaspoon salt, ¼ teaspoon black pepper, onions, sugar and 1 teaspoon thyme to pan. Cook 20 minutes or until onions are tender and golden brown, stirring occasionally. Add garlic, carrots and celery; cook 5 minutes, stirring occasionally. Preheat oven to 325°. Place beef on top of onion mixture, pour wine mixture over beef. Cover and place in oven. Bake 1 hour and 45 minutes.

While beef mixture cooks, place potatoes in a large bowl. Add ¾ teaspoon salt, ¼ teaspoon thyme, oil, oregano and red pepper; toss to coat. Arrange in a single layer on a jelly-roll pan coated with cooking spray. Remove beef from oven and turn over. Place potatoes on lower rack in oven. Cover beef, return to oven. Bake potatoes and beef at 325°, 45 minutes or until beef is tender. Remove beef from oven, cover and keep warm. Increase oven temperature to 425°. Place potatoes on middle rack in oven, bake 15 minutes or until crisp and edges are browned. Remove beef from pan, cut across the grain into thin slices. Serve with onion mixture and potatoes. Sprinkle with parsley.

Worth the Effort

Poultry

Manna would assume any flavor one wished for when eating it. So that if one merely thought, "I wish to eat roast chicken," it immediately tasted like roast chicken!

(Sh'mos Rabbah, 25,3)

Just a Reminder...
green = pareve   red = meat   blue = dairy

Super Easy Chicken

Yields: 6-8 servings

3-4 pound whole chicken cut up or 3-4 pounds boneless chicken breasts

1 (16-ounce) can cranberry sauce, whole berry

1 (16-ounce) bottle French salad dressing

1 package onion soup mix

1 teaspoon garlic powder

Preheat oven to 350°. Mix cranberry sauce, French salad dressing, onion soup mix and garlic powder. Pour over chicken and bake 1½ hours, basting chicken frequently with the sauce. If using boneless chicken breasts, cook only 30-45 minutes.

To vary this recipe, substitute apricot jam or orange marmalade instead of cranberry sauce.

Quick n Easy

Turkey Burgers

Yields: 8 servings

2 pounds ground turkey

2 eggs

½ cup flavored bread crumbs

1 garlic clove, minced, or 1 tablespoon garlic powder

1 teaspoon curry powder

Salt and pepper to taste

Preheat oven to 325°. Mix all ingredients in bowl until blended. Roll into 8 burgers. Place on a broiler pan and cook 10 minutes each side.

The knife and fork revolutionized meat etiquette in the 16th and 17th centuries, but chicken, cut in pieces, was and still is spared this formality.

OVEN-FRIED CHICKEN

Yields: 6 servings

4 tablespoons margarine
½ cup all-purpose flour
1 teaspoon salt
1 teaspoon paprika

¼ teaspoon pepper
2½-3-pound broiler-fryer chicken, cut up

Preheat oven to 425°. Melt margarine in 13 x 9 x 2-inch pan in oven. Mix flour, salt, paprika and pepper. Coat chicken pieces with flour mixture. Place skin side down in pan. Bake uncovered 30 minutes. Turn chicken; bake until thickest pieces are done, about 30 minutes longer.

Crunchy Oven-Fried Chicken: Substitute 1 cup corn flake crumbs for ½ cup flour. Dip chicken in 4 tablespoons margarine, melted, before coating with crumb mixture.

FINGER LICKIN'
SOUTHERN FRIED CHICKEN

Yields: 6 servings

½ cup all-purpose flour
1 teaspoon salt
1 teaspoon paprika
¼ teaspoon pepper

2½-3 pounds broiler-fryer chicken, cut up
Vegetable oil

Mix flour, salt, paprika and pepper. Coat chicken pieces with flour mixture. Heat oil (¼-inch) in 12-inch skillet over medium-high heat until hot. Cook chicken in oil until light brown on all sides, about 10 minutes; reduce heat. Fry chicken in oil until crisp, turn once and fry until thickest pieces are done.

SWEET AND TASTY CHICKEN BREASTS

Yields: 6-8 servings

6-8 boneless chicken breasts, cleaned
    and dried
½ teaspoon vegetable oil
1 (15-ounce) jar of apricot preserves

1 cup orange juice
¼ teaspoon curry powder
¼ cup honey
2 cloves garlic, crushed

Place chicken in a lightly oiled baking pan. Combine remaining ingredients in a bowl and microwave 45 seconds on high. Stir again and pour over chicken. Marinate 1 hour, turning the breasts after 30 minutes. Preheat oven to 350° and bake chicken breasts 20-25 minutes. Do not overcook. Serve with rice.

SWEET AND STICKY CORNISH HENS

Yields: 4 servings

4 Cornish hens, at room temperature,
    cut in half
2 teaspoons prepared mustard

1 tablespoon dry mustard
½ cup apricot preserves
½ cup apricot nectar

Preheat oven to 425°. Line a shallow roasting pan with heavy duty foil and place hens on it, skin side up. In a small bowl, stir together rest of ingredients. With a brush, dab glaze over the hens. Roast 45 minutes, basting every 15 minutes. Hens are done when juice runs clear.

TURKEY CHILI FOR A CROWD

Yields: 25-30 servings

2¾ pounds ground turkey

4¼ pounds hot turkey sausage, removed from casing

4 tablespoons olive oil

2 large white onions (not sweet), chopped

4 red peppers, diced

6 large garlic cloves, chopped

2 (28-ounce) cans diced tomatoes, undrained

2 small cans green chilies, drained

4 (15-ounce) cans white beans, drained and rinsed

2 cups dry red wine, such as Cabernet or Merlot

2 tablespoons chili powder

3 tablespoons oregano

2½ teaspoons salt

2 teaspoons pepper

1 tablespoon cumin

4 tablespoons parsley, dried

Brown ground turkey and turkey sausage in a large pan until cooked. Add rest of ingredients. Bring to boil and lower heat to simmer. Cook 45 minutes to 1 hour uncovered.

Great for a large crowd. Recipe can be cut in half. Freezes well.

Chicken Piccata

Yields: 6-8 servings

2 pounds chicken breasts, skinned, boned, and flattened to ¼-inch thickness
Salt and pepper, to taste
2 cups flour for dredging
3 tablespoons margarine

1 tablespoon olive oil
2 cloves garlic, minced
½ pound mushrooms
¼ cup capers
2 tablespoons fresh lemon juice
½ cup dry white wine

Sprinkle chicken with salt and pepper. Dredge in flour. Melt margarine in skillet over medium-high heat, add olive oil and garlic and sauté briefly. Add chicken breasts and sauté 1-2 minutes on each side; set aside. Add mushrooms and capers to skillet; sauté 2-4 minutes. Add lemon juice and wine. Return chicken to pan. Cook until juices run clear.

You can use 2 cups of matzo meal instead of flour if you prefer.

Roast Chicken

Yields: 8-10 servings

2 whole chickens
⅓ cup soy sauce
⅓ cup maple syrup

Granulated garlic, to taste
Black pepper, coarse grind, to taste
Paprika, to taste

Preheat oven to 450°. Rinse chickens and place breast side down in roasting pan that is slightly larger than the chickens (too large a pan causes the juices to evaporate). Mix soy sauce and maple syrup together and drizzle over chickens. Sprinkle a fine layer of granulated garlic over chickens, followed by pepper to taste. Sprinkle generously with paprika. Reduce oven temperature to 350°. Bake 20 minutes per pound of chicken until caramel brown. No need to baste or turn.

Whole roasted chickens are more tender and juicy. If baking parts, reduce baking time to about an hour.

HAWAIIAN CHICKEN

Yield: 8-12 servings

4 pounds chicken, cut up
1 large onion, chopped
3 tablespoons canola oil
14 ounces water
14 ounces ketchup
4 tablespoons white vinegar

1 cup brown sugar
½ tablespoon garlic powder
½ tablespoon onion powder
4 tablespoons soy sauce
1 (20-ounce) can pineapple chunks, drained

Preheat oven to 350°. Sauté onion in hot oil until golden brown. Add water, ketchup, vinegar and brown sugar. Heat until sugar dissolves. Season chicken with garlic powder and onion powder. Place in greased casserole dish and pour sauce over it. Sprinkle with soy sauce. Bake uncovered 1 hour and 15 minutes. Baste every 10 minutes. Add pineapple chunks and bake 15 more minutes.

CHICKEN FRICASSEE

Yields: 12 servings

2 pounds ground beef
1 large onion, chopped
24-36 chicken wings or drumettes
Salt, to taste

Pepper, to taste
Paprika, to taste and color
Vegetable oil for cooking

Form ground beef into 1-inch meatballs and bake 15 minutes at 350°. Sauté onion in oil in large pot until soft. Add chicken wings (cut in half, tips discarded) or drumettes to onions. Sprinkle with salt, pepper and paprika. Cover with water and cook 45 minutes. Add meatballs and simmer 1½ hours over medium heat. Serve over rice.

Since the
early Middle Ages, European
Jews have eaten a variety of poultry, likely
because raising geese and poultry was
a traditional Jewish occupation.

RAISIN ALMOND CHICKEN

Yields: 4-6 servings

6 large chicken parts with skin and
    bones
2 large onions, halved and sliced
½ teaspoon garlic salt
¼ teaspoon pepper

6 tablespoons margarine
1 (10-ounce jar) honey
½ box white raisins
1 cup white wine
1 (12-ounce) package sliced almonds

Preheat oven to 375°. Lay chicken parts on top of sliced onions in a baking dish and season well with garlic salt and pepper. Melt 4 tablespoons margarine and add to honey. Combine well and pour evenly over chicken. Bake 1 hour uncovered, basting often. Simmer raisins in wine until plumped. Sauté almonds in 2 tablespoons margarine until golden and mix with raisins. Pour on chicken just prior to serving.

ARROZ CON POLLO VALENCIANA

Yields: 4-6 servings

2½ pounds frying chicken, cut into
    pieces
¼ cup olive oil
2 cloves garlic, chopped
1 onion, chopped
1 green pepper, chopped
1 bay leaf

1 (14½-ounce) can whole cooked
    tomatoes
1 tablespoon salt
1 cup chicken broth
½ teaspoon saffron, ground
1 cup rice, uncooked

Preheat oven to 350°. Heat olive oil and brown chicken pieces on all sides in an oven-safe baking dish on top of stove. Remove chicken and juices. Add garlic, onion and green pepper to baking dish and sauté until onion is golden. Add bay leaf and tomatoes; return chicken to baking dish and add chicken broth. When broth boils, add salt, saffron and rice. Cover baking dish and bake in oven 20 minutes or until rice is tender. Garnish.

Garnish: strips of pimiento, ½ cup cooked green peas, 4-6 asparagus tips, chopped parsley.

LEMON CHICKEN STIR-FRY

Yields: 8 servings

2 tablespoons soy sauce
2 tablespoons cornstarch
2 pounds boneless chicken breasts,
    cut in strips
3 tablespoons lemon juice
2 tablespoons sugar
1 teaspoon grated lemon rind

4 tablespoons oil
4 green onions, sliced
1 carrot, sliced
1 green pepper, cut in strips
1 red pepper, cut in strips
2 teaspoons minced garlic

Combine soy sauce and cornstarch in a large bowl; stir until smooth. Add chicken; toss well and set aside. Combine lemon juice, sugar and lemon rind and stir well; set aside. Heat oil in large skillet over medium heat. Add onions, carrots, peppers and garlic; cover and cook 2 minutes. Remove vegetables from skillet and cover to keep warm. Add chicken mixture to hot oil; stir-fry 4 minutes or until done. Stir in lemon mixture. Cover, reduce heat and simmer 2 minutes. Add vegetable mixture and cook until heated thoroughly.

A family favorite for Pesach. Substitute potato starch for cornstarch.

CHICKEN WITH ARTICHOKES AND WHITE WINE

Yields: 4 servings

4 skinless, boneless chicken breast
    halves
2 teaspoons all-purpose flour
4 tablespoons margarine
2 (9-ounce) packages frozen artichoke
    hearts, thawed

1 cup chopped onion
2 teaspoons Italian seasoning
1¾ cups chicken broth
1 cup dry white wine
Salt and pepper, to taste

Sprinkle chicken with salt and pepper; dust with flour. Melt margarine in heavy, large skillet over medium-high heat. Add chicken; sauté until brown, about 3 minutes per side. Transfer chicken to plate. Add artichokes, onion and Italian seasoning to skillet. Sauté until onion is tender. Add broth and wine, boil until liquid is reduced by half, about 8 minutes. Return chicken and accumulated juices to skillet. Cover, reduce heat to medium-low. Simmer until chicken is cooked through and artichokes are tender. Season to taste with salt and pepper.

CRUNCHY OVEN-BAKED CHICKEN WITH SPEEDY APRICOT SAUCE

Yields: 4 servings

CHICKEN

4 (4-ounce) boneless, skinless chicken breasts
¼ teaspoon salt
⅛ teaspoon ground black pepper

2¾ cups corn flakes cereal
½ teaspoon dried thyme leaves
¼ teaspoon dried tarragon leaves
1 egg white

SAUCE

3 tablespoons apricot preserves
1 tablespoon Dijon mustard

2 tablespoons chicken broth
1 teaspoon soy sauce

Preheat oven to 350°.

Chicken: Lightly spray baking dish with nonstick vegetable coating; set aside. Pound chicken to an even thickness. Sprinkle lightly with salt and pepper. Place cereal in food processor, blender or heavy-duty plastic bag. Add thyme leaves and tarragon; pulverize together until cereal crumbs are very fine. Place egg white in one shallow dish and cereal crumbs in another. Dip chicken in egg white and dredge in crumbs. Fold thin, pointed ends of chicken under thick end to form a rough square shape; place in prepared dish. Sprinkle with leftover crumbs. Bake until chicken is firm to the touch and opaque, 35-40 minutes.

Sauce: While chicken is cooking, combine apricot preserves, mustard and chicken broth in a microwave-safe dish. Stirring after each 30-second interval, microwave on high until preserves have melted and sauce is hot. Stir in soy sauce.

Serve sauce on side or drizzle lightly over chicken.

CHICKEN WITH DRIED FRUIT AND PINE NUTS

Yields: 4 servings

1 whole chicken, cut up
1 tablespoon olive oil
½ cup pitted prunes
½ cup dried apricots
¼ cup dried tart cherries

2 tablespoons pine nuts
½ cup tawny port or sweet white wine
1 medium cinnamon stick
½ cup chicken stock or low sodium
   broth

Preheat oven to 350°. Place chicken in a baking dish, cover and bake until cooked through, 1-1½ hours. Reserve juice. Heat olive oil in a large skillet. Add prunes, apricots, cherries and pine nuts and cook over moderate heat, stirring, until the pine nuts are golden and the apricots are browned in spots, about 3 minutes. Add the port or wine and cinnamon stick, cook over moderate heat until syrupy, about 5 minutes. Add stock and juice from the baking dish and bring to a boil. Meanwhile, in a large nonstick skillet, brown the chicken pieces over high heat until the skin is golden and crisp, 5-7 minutes. Scrape the dried fruit sauce and liquid into the skillet with the chicken and bring to a boil, turning chicken until nicely coated with sauce, about 1 minute.

CRUSTED TURKEY PATTIES WITH HONEY MUSTARD

Yields: 4-5 servings

COATING

½ cup chopped pecans
3 cups toasted corn cereal
¼ cup mayonnaise

1 tablespoon honey
2 tablespoons Dijon mustard
½ teaspoon dry mustard

TURKEY PATTIES

1 pound turkey breasts, cut into chunks
2 medium garlic cloves, peeled
5 large green onions cut in 1-inch pieces
2 tablespoons mayonnaise
1 teaspoon honey

2 tablespoons Dijon mustard
1¼ teaspoons dried tarragon
½ teaspoon salt
½ teaspoon black pepper, freshly ground

Preheat oven to 425°.

Coating: In a food processor with the metal blade, chop pecans into small pieces. Add cereal and pulse until mixture is finely chopped. Remove to a shallow bowl. In another shallow bowl, stir together mayonnaise, honey and mustards.

Turkey Patties: In same processor bowl, mince garlic and green onions and pulse to chop. Chop turkey in processor and add mayonnaise, honey, mustard, tarragon, salt and pepper. Pulse to combine. Shape into 10 (2½-inch) patties. Dip both sides into mustard mixture and then into crumbs.

Place rack on top rung of oven. Place patties on greased baking sheet and bake 8-10 minutes.

Fish

The manna would only
taste like the special taste of fish
on Shabbat and holidays.

(Sefer Haparshiot, Parshat B'haaloscha)

Just a Reminder...
green = pareve   red = meat   blue = dairy

TUSCAN BAKED FISH

Yields: 6 servings

2 pounds flounder or sole filets
Butter
1 cup shredded mozzarella cheese
1 large tomato, thinly sliced

½ teaspoon dried oregano
½ teaspoon granulated garlic powder
Salt and ground pepper

Preheat oven to 375°. Butter large baking dish. Rinse filets in salted water and pat dry. Arrange in single layer in dish. Sprinkle with cheese and cover with tomato slices. Dust with oregano, garlic, salt and pepper to taste. Bake until fish is opaque, 15-20 minutes.

Best if served on a heated platter.

FLOUNDER OREGANATA

Yields: 4 servings

4 flounder filets
½ cup seasoned bread crumbs
1 cup grated Parmesan cheese
1 cup lemon juice

½ cup olive oil
4 garlic cloves, crushed
2 teaspoons oregano

Mix together bread crumbs, Parmesan cheese, lemon juice, olive oil, garlic and oregano to form a paste. Consistency should be easily spreadable. Spread on top of filets. Broil fish on bottom rack of oven 7 minutes. If fish is brown on top and not cooked on the bottom, change oven to bake at 350° for several minutes.

SESAME CRUSTED TUNA

Yields: 4 servings

4 (1-inch) thick tuna filets
½ cup sesame oil
¼ cup soy sauce
½ teaspoon garlic powder

3 dashes hot sauce
Black and white sesame seeds
Vegetable oil for cooking

Marinate tuna in sesame oil, soy sauce, garlic powder and hot sauce. Refrigerate up to 1 hour. Remove tuna from marinade and coat with sesame seeds. Coat pan with oil and sear filets 2-5 minutes each side to preferred doneness.

SALMON LOAF WITH DILL SAUCE

Yields: 8 servings

SALMON
1 (15-ounce) can salmon, drained and
    flaked
1 (10½-ounce) can condensed cream of
    mushroom soup
2 eggs, beaten

1 cup dry bread crumbs
½ cup mayonnaise
½ cup chopped onions
¼ cup chopped green pepper

SAUCE
½ cup mayonnaise
½ cup sour cream
½ cup chopped cucumber

2 tablespoons chopped onion
½ teaspoon dill

Preheat oven to 350°.

Salmon: Mix all ingredients together and put in a greased loaf pan. Bake 50 minutes.

Sauce: Mix all ingredients together and use as a topping.

Sea Bass with Roasted Pepper Salsa

Yields: 4 servings

FISH
4 sea bass filets
Salt, pepper, garlic, thyme to taste

1 cup white wine

SALSA
2 red peppers
2 yellow peppers
2 tablespoons fresh parsley, chopped
1 tablespoon olive oil

1 tablespoon red wine vinegar
1 garlic clove, minced
½ cup kalamata olives, pitted and sliced

Preheat oven to 350°.

Fish: Place sea bass in a baking dish, season with spices. Pour in wine and bake 25 minutes.

Roasted Peppers: Cut peppers in half. Discard seeds and ribs. Place peppers under broiler until skin is blackened. Place in paper bag 30 minutes, take out, remove skin and dice them.

Salsa: Mix together ingredients and serve with sea bass.

GRILLED SALMON

Yields: 4 servings

4 (6-ounce) salmon filets
¼ cup olive oil
¼ cup soy sauce

2 tablespoons tarragon
½ fresh lemon, squeezed
Pepper, to taste

Mix all ingredients except salmon. Marinate salmon in the mixture for 30 minutes to 1 hour. Grill or broil skin side down 10-12 minutes.

ASIAN SALMON

Yields: 4-6 servings

6 (6-ounce) salmon filets
⅓ cup honey
¾ tablespoon fresh ginger, minced
⅛ cup dark soy sauce
⅛ cup white wine
1 tablespoon whole grain mustard
2 tablespoons parsley, chopped

Juice of ½ lemon
1 tablespoon vegetable oil
1 tablespoon vinegar
Salt and pepper, to taste
¼ teaspoon crushed red pepper
Sliced green onions for topping

Preheat oven to 400°. In a blender combine all ingredients except salmon. Pour over salmon and bake uncovered 20-25 minutes.

Grilled Tilapia with Lime and Basil

Yields: 4 servings

4 filets fresh tilapia, about 1 pound
4 tablespoons canola oil
Zest of 2 limes
2 tablespoons fresh lime juice

1 tablespoon minced fresh basil
2 teaspoons bourbon
1 teaspoon salt
Freshly ground pepper

For marinade, combine all ingredients, except fish, in a large plastic storage bag. Add fish, coating with marinade. Seal bag, refrigerate. Marinate 30 minutes, occasionally turning bag to coat fish. Heat grill or grill pan. Remove tilapia from marinade; pour marinade into a small saucepan. Cook filets on grill or grill pan until opaque, about 3 minutes per side. Boil marinade. Remove from heat and serve.

Fish

CHILEAN SEA BASS IN PUTTANESCA SAUCE

Yields: 4 servings

4 sea bass filets or any mild white fish
2-3 garlic cloves, chopped
2 tablespoons olive oil
1 (28-ounce) can diced tomatoes, undrained
1 (14-ounce) can artichokes, drained, quartered
½ cup dry white wine

2 teaspoons chopped fresh basil
2 teaspoons oregano
2 tablespoons chopped fresh parsley
½ cup kalamata olives, sliced and drained
Salt and pepper, to taste
3 tablespoons capers

Sauté garlic in olive oil. Add tomatoes and all other ingredients except fish and capers. Cook uncovered 20 minutes. Add fish, cover and continue to cook 15-20 minutes or until done. Add capers about 5 minutes before fish is finished.

Serve over roasted garlic couscous, cooked according to package directions.

SALMON STEAKS IN ORANGE-HONEY MARINADE

Yields: 4 servings

4 (6-ounce) salmon filets
⅓ cup orange juice
⅓ cup soy sauce
3 tablespoons peanut oil

3 tablespoons ketchup
1 tablespoon honey
½ teaspoon ground ginger
1 garlic clove, crushed

Mix all ingredients except salmon filets. Place filets in shallow glass dish. Pour marinade over filets, cover and refrigerate 2-4 hours. Grill filets on uncovered grill 5 minutes. Turn filets, brush with marinade and grill 5 minutes longer or until salmon flakes easily when tested with fork.

When broiling in oven, broil salmon on both sides until it is cooked all the way through.

CRISP ROASTED SALMON

Yields: 12-14 servings

1 (3½-4 pound) salmon filet, skin on,
    at room temperature
Salt and black pepper, to taste
3 tablespoons extra virgin olive oil
4 shallots, coarsely chopped

1 tablespoon dried dill
12 fresh thyme sprigs
6 fresh rosemary sprigs
½ cup dry vermouth or
    other dry white wine

Preheat broiler. Sprinkle flesh side of salmon with salt and pepper and rub with olive oil. Place shallots, dill, thyme and rosemary in shallow roasting pan. Place salmon on top of herbs, skin side up, and pour vermouth around salmon. Broil 6 inches from heat source 12-15 minutes, until skin is charred and crisp and flesh is cooked through (pierce fish with a sharp knife to check). Flip salmon over on serving platter so that skin side is down; slice and serve.

Can be kept warm under aluminum foil for an hour or so before serving. It is also terrific cold. Wait until last minute to slice.

PAN-ROASTED ROCKFISH WITH FRIED CAPERS

Yields: 4 servings

4 rockfish filets (about 2 pounds)
2 tablespoons capers
2 tablespoons olive oil plus more for
    frying

1 garlic clove, crushed
Sea salt and freshly ground pepper
1 lemon, cut into wedges

Preheat oven to 400°. Drain and pat dry capers. Heat ½ inch oil in small saucepan over medium-high heat. Add capers and sauté until brown on the edges, 30-60 seconds. Drain on paper towel. Pour 2 tablespoons oil in large nonstick sauté pan. Place over medium-high heat. Add garlic clove. Season fish with salt and pepper. When garlic bubbles on the edges, lay fish in pan, skin side down. Sauté until browned on the bottom, 4-5 minutes. Put pan in oven and roast until fish is just cooked through, 5-8 minutes. Serve sprinkled with capers and lemons.

GRILLED TUNA WITH BRUSCHETTA

Yields: 4 servings

TUNA STEAKS
4 tuna filets

Olive oil

Salt and pepper

Garlic powder

BRUSCHETTA
10 plum tomatoes, diced

¼ cup kalamata olives, pitted and sliced

2 teaspoons capers, drained

½ Vidalia onion, diced

2 tablespoons fresh basil, chopped

1 lemon, squeezed

1 tablespoon olive oil

3 garlic cloves, crushed

Salt and pepper, to taste

Tuna Steaks: Rub tuna with olive oil and season with salt, pepper and garlic powder to desired taste. Grill 2 minutes on each side for medium rare.

Bruschetta: Mix all ingredients together. Taste for extra seasoning. Serve over grilled tuna.

For a wonderful appetizer, add roasted red peppers and serve with crostini or garlic crisps.

After leaving Egypt, one of the foods the Jews longed for was fish, which they had had in abundance.

BAKED SEA BASS
WITH CURRIED PECAN TOPPING

Yields: 4 servings

4 (6-ounce) sea bass filets
  (1-1¼ inches thick)
⅓ cup finely chopped pecans
⅓ cup fresh French bread crumbs
1 tablespoon finely chopped onion
1 garlic clove, crushed

½ teaspoon ground cumin
Pinch of cayenne pepper
1 teaspoon curry powder
1 tablespoon vegetable oil
1 egg white

Preheat oven to 350°. Mix pecans, bread crumbs, onion, garlic, cumin, cayenne pepper and curry powder in an 8 x 8 x 2-inch glass baking dish. Add oil; stir to blend. Bake until mixture is light golden, about 8 minutes. Transfer to plate and cool. Increase oven temperature to 450°.

Beat egg white in a medium bowl until foamy. Dip fish filets one at a time into egg white, then into pecan mixture, coating both sides. Arrange fish in same baking dish. Sprinkle with salt and pepper. Press any excess pecan mixture atop filets. Bake until fish is opaque in center, about 12 minutes, and serve.

This dish comes together quickly, making it ideal for a weeknight dinner. Just add some steamed rice or sautéed baby potatoes and a tossed green salad.

Dairy
and
Brunch

The first manna fell on Sunday,
31 days after the Exodus from Egypt. …
Also, the manna collection hours were
during the first three hours of morning.

(Sefer Haparshiot, Parshas B'shalach)

WAFFLES

Yields: 4 servings

2 eggs
2 cups all-purpose flour*
½ cup melted margarine
1¾ cups milk

1 tablespoon sugar
4 teaspoons baking powder
½ teaspoon salt

*If using self-rising flour, omit baking powder and salt

Heat waffle iron. Beat eggs with hand beater until fluffy; beat in remaining ingredients just until smooth. Pour batter from cup or pitcher onto center of hot waffle iron. Bake until steaming stops, according to manufacturer's instructions. Remove waffles carefully.

Blueberry Waffles: *Sprinkle 2-4 tablespoons fresh or frozen blueberries (thawed and well-drained) over batter immediately after pouring it onto iron.*

Whole Wheat Waffles: *Substitute whole wheat flour for all-purpose flour and packed brown sugar for granulated sugar. If desired, sprinkle 2 tablespoons wheat germ or sesame seed over batter immediately after pouring it onto the iron.*

Dairy and Brunch

Fruit Noodle Kugel

Yields: 10-12 servings

PUDDING

1 pound noodles, cooked and drained
½ cup sugar
1 cup soy milk
1 cup apricot nectar

3 tablespoons margarine, melted
3 eggs
1 teaspoon vanilla
Dash of cinnamon

TOPPING

1 tablespoon margarine
¼ cup cornflake crumbs

½ teaspoon cinnamon
1 can sliced peaches, drained

Preheat oven to 375°.

Pudding: Mix all ingredients and bake 40 minutes.

Topping: Combine all ingredients except peaches.

Crumble topping over kugel. Add peaches. Bake 30 minutes.

BASIC MATZO BREI

Yields: 4 servings

2 matzos
2 eggs

Butter
Salt and pepper, to taste

Crumble matzo into medium-size pieces and place in a bowl. Pour boiling water over broken matzo. Drain well. Beat eggs and add salt and pepper to taste. Mix with softened matzo. In a small frying pan, melt butter and pour into matzo egg mixture. Fry like a pancake until brown on both sides.

For a sweeter taste, serve with cinnamon and sugar.

TUNA QUICHE

Yields: 6 servings

1 (8-inch) pre-made pie crust
1 (7-ounce) can tuna in water, drained
1 cup evaporated milk
1 egg

6 ounces sharp Cheddar cheese, grated
Salt and pepper, to taste
1 can fried onion rings, crushed

Preheat oven to 375°. Flake tuna. Beat egg and milk together and pour into tuna. Add grated cheese, salt and pepper and mix well. Pour into pie crust. Sprinkle with crushed onion rings and bake 30-35 minutes.

Strawberry French Toast

Yields: 4 servings

12 (½-inch) thick slices French bread
    with crust
1½ cups sliced strawberries
1 egg, lightly beaten
2 egg whites, lightly beaten
¾ cup milk

2 tablespoons honey
½ teaspoon pure vanilla extract
¼ teaspoon cinnamon
¼ cup sliced almonds
1 teaspoon sugar

Arrange half the bread slices in the bottom of an 8 x 8 x 2-inch baking dish coated with cooking spray. Top bread with a layer of strawberries and then the remaining bread. Combine eggs, egg whites, milk, honey, vanilla and cinnamon. Pour slowly over bread to coat evenly. Cover and chill 8-24 hours. Preheat oven to 425°. Uncover bread; sprinkle with almonds and sugar. Bake 5 minutes. Reduce temperature to 325°. Bake 20-25 minutes or until knife inserted near center comes out clean and top is slightly browned. Let stand 5 minutes. Serve immediately.

Prepare Ahead of Time

SALMON CRUNCH PIE

Yields: 6 servings

WHOLE WHEAT CRUST
1½ cups whole wheat flour
1 cup sharp Cheddar cheese, shredded
½ teaspoon salt
½ teaspoon paprika
½ cup butter
⅓ cup almonds, finely chopped

SALMON MIXTURE
1 (15-ounce) can red salmon
3 eggs, beaten
1 cup sour cream
½ cup sharp Cheddar cheese, shredded
¼ cup mayonnaise
1 tablespoon grated onion
3 drops hot pepper sauce
¼ teaspoon dill weed

Preheat oven to 400°.

Whole Wheat Crust: Combine flour, cheese, salt and paprika in food processor. Cut in butter until mixture resembles coarse crumbs. Add almonds. Save 1 cup crumb mixture for topping. Press remaining mixture into 9-inch pie plate.

Salmon Mixture: Drain, remove bones and flake salmon, reserving liquid. Add to salmon: reserved liquid, eggs, sour cream, cheese, mayonnaise and seasonings. Mix thoroughly. Turn into pie plate lined with crust. Sprinkle with reserved crumbs. Bake 45 minutes.

PECAN NOODLE PUDDING

Yields: 14-16 servings

¼ cup butter
1 cup brown sugar
1 (6-ounce) package whole pecans
2 (8-ounce) packages broad noodles, cooked

4 eggs
½ cup butter, melted
½ teaspoon cinnamon
⅔ cup sugar
1 teaspoon salt

Preheat oven to 350°. Melt butter in large ring mold, press sugar in butter and press whole pecans in mixture. Refrigerate 30 minutes. Mix and pour rest of ingredients into chilled mold. Bake 1 hour. You can also bake ½ hour and freeze, then bake ½ hour before serving.

BROCCOLI CHEESE BAKE

Yields: 6-8 servings

1 cup chopped onion
2 teaspoons garlic, finely chopped
1 tablespoon olive oil
2 cups frozen broccoli florets, defrosted and drained
1 tablespoon fresh basil, chopped
4 egg whites

⅓ cup milk
2 tablespoons grated Parmesan cheese
1 cup grated Cheddar cheese
1 ready-made pie shell
¼ cup seasoned bread crumbs
Cooking spray

Preheat oven to 350°. Sauté onion and garlic in olive oil until tender. Add broccoli and basil. Cook, covered, for 10 minutes. In separate bowl, mix egg white, milk, Parmesan cheese and Cheddar cheese. Pour half of cheese mixture into pie shell. Add broccoli mixture. Pour remaining cheese mixture on top of broccoli. Sprinkle bread crumbs on top. Spray with cooking spray. Bake uncovered 25-30 minutes or until set.

"Pasta" became the
Jewish *"lokshen"* through the Italian
presence in the royal courts of Poland
where it was called *"loksyn."*

SWEET KUGEL

Yields: 10 servings

TOPPING

2 cups cornflakes, crushed

1 cup brown sugar

2 sticks butter, melted separately

KUGEL

9 eggs

1½ pounds medium noodles, cooked
   and drained

1½ pounds small curd cottage cheese

3 ounces cream cheese, softened

3 cups milk

1 cup sugar

1 tablespoon salt

2 tablespoons vanilla extract

½ stick melted butter

2 tablespoons cinnamon

1½ cups golden raisins

Preheat oven to 350°.

Topping: combine cornflake crumbs, brown sugar and 1 stick melted butter. Set aside.

Kugel: Beat eggs. Mix all ingredients for kugel, pour into greased 15 x 10½ x 2-inch pan. Scatter topping over kugel. Drizzle with remaining stick of melted butter. Bake 1 hour.

CALZONE

Yields: 4 servings

¾ cup cottage cheese
¼ cup cream cheese
3 tablespoons grated Parmesan cheese
½ cup sour cream
1 package frozen chopped spinach,
  defrosted and squeezed dry
1 (7-ounce) jar roasted red peppers

1 teaspoon garlic powder
¼ teaspoon pepper
1 refrigerated pizza crust
¼ cup mozzarella cheese, shredded
¼ cup Cheddar cheese, shredded
1½ cups pasta sauce

Preheat oven to 425°. Combine cottage cheese, cream cheese and Parmesan cheese with sour cream, mix in blender until well blended. Add spinach, red peppers, garlic powder and pepper. Spread pizza crust on a 14 x 10-inch baking sheet. On half of crust, spread mixture and sprinkle with the last two cheeses. Fold over and squeeze edges together to close. Bake 15 minutes. Let cool 5 minutes. Cover with pasta sauce.

UNBEATABLE SPINACH QUICHE

Yields: 6 servings

1 (9-inch) pie crust
1 (9-ounce) package frozen spinach,
  chopped and well drained
2 tablespoons margarine, melted
1 cup cottage cheese
3 eggs, beaten

½ cup half-and-half cream or canned
  milk
½ cup Parmesan cheese
Pinch of nutmeg
¼ teaspoon each salt, pepper and sugar

Preheat oven to 450°. Bake pie shell 8 minutes. Blend margarine, cottage cheese, eggs and half-and-half or milk. Add remaining ingredients, mix well and blend in spinach. Pour into pie shell. Reduce temperature to 375°. Bake 1 hour or until filling is set. Let stand 5-10 minutes before cutting.

EGG SOUFFLÉ

Yields: 8-12 servings

12 large eggs
½ cup all-purpose flour
½-1 teaspoon salt
1 pint creamed cottage cheese
1 pound sharp Cheddar cheese,
    shredded
½ cup butter, melted
1 teaspoon baking powder

½ green pepper, diced
2 tablespoons parsley, chopped
½ large onion, grated
½ pound mushrooms, sliced and
    sautéed in additional butter and
    drained
2 medium tomatoes, thinly sliced

Preheat oven to 350°. Beat eggs until fluffy; add a little egg to flour and mix until smooth. Pour back into eggs and add rest of ingredients except sliced tomatoes. Stir by hand. Pour into greased 13 x 9 x 2-inch baking dish. Lay tomatoes on top. Bake 45 minutes or until firm.

Chef's Choice

Dairy and Brunch

Blinchiki, the ancestors of blintzes, were brought to the United States by Ukrainian Jews.

BLINTZ CASSEROLE

Yields: 12 servings

FILLING
2 pounds ricotta cheese
8 ounces cream cheese, softened
2 eggs
¼ cup sugar
⅛ teaspoon salt
¼ cup lemon juice

BATTER
8 ounces butter, melted
½ cup sugar
2 eggs
1 cup flour
3 teaspoons baking powder
½ teaspoon salt
¼ cup milk
1 teaspoon vanilla

Preheat oven to 350°.

Filling: Place all filling ingredients in an electric mixer bowl and blend well. Set aside.

Batter: Mix batter ingredients by hand. Spoon half of batter into greased 9 x 13 x 2-inch pan. Top this with filling; spread, but do not mix. Spread remaining batter over filling. Bake 1½ hours.

Brunch Eggs

Yields: 10-12 servings

8 ounces Monterey Jack cheese, grated
16 ounces cottage cheese
6 eggs, beaten
½ cup margarine, melted
1 cup milk

1 cup biscuit baking mix
½ cup mushrooms, sliced, optional
1 (6-ounce) container French fried onions

Preheat oven to 350°. Combine cheeses, eggs, margarine, milk, biscuit baking mix and mushrooms. Pour into a greased 13 x 9 x 2-inch pan. Sprinkle onions on top. Bake 35-40 minutes.

Looking for something different? This is it-and it's delicious.

Rustic Lasagna

Yields: 8 servings

1 package lasagna noodles
2 (15-ounce) cans tomato sauce
1 teaspoon minced garlic
1 teaspoon oregano
1 (10-ounce) package chopped frozen spinach, thawed and squeezed dry
1 cup shredded carrots

2 eggs
1 pound ricotta cheese
½ cup grated Romano cheese
½ cup grated Parmesan cheese
1 cup grated mozzarella cheese
Salt and pepper to taste

Preheat oven to 350°. Cook noodles in boiling water. Combine tomato sauce, garlic and oregano in a small bowl. Set aside. Combine spinach, carrots, eggs, ricotta cheese, Romano cheese, Parmesan cheese and salt and pepper in a medium bowl. In a 9 x 13 x 2-inch pan, spread ½ cup of sauce, a layer of noodles, ½ cup of filling, and so on, alternating until complete, ending with a layer of sauce. Top with mozzarella cheese. Bake 45 minutes. Allow to cool 10 minutes before slicing.

RASPBERRY KUGEL

Yields: 12-15 servings

3 cups long-grain white rice
16 ounces frozen raspberries
   (separate berries but do not thaw)
7 large eggs

1 cup margarine, melted
1¼ cups sugar
2 tablespoons vanilla
Sugar and cinnamon for topping

Preheat oven to 350°. Cook rice according to package directions. Beat eggs in large mixing bowl until well blended. Beat in margarine, sugar and vanilla. Combine with cooked rice and pour into greased 13 x 9 x 2-inch baking pan. Place berries on top, pressing down slightly into batter to prevent burning. Sprinkle with sugar and cinnamon. Bake uncovered 1¼ hours.

Substitute frozen blueberries or strawberries for variety.

King David,
going out to his brothers
fighting the Philistines, brings them
cheeses. (Samuel 1, 17:18)

MEDITERRANEAN STRATA LITE

Yields: 8-12 servings

6-8 slices sourdough or French bread cut into 1-inch cubes
1 (10-ounce) package frozen chopped spinach, thawed and squeezed dry
1 tablespoon dried basil
1 (14½-ounce) can tomatoes, drained

2½ cups reduced fat shredded mozzarella cheese (can substitute Swiss or Romano cheese)
¾ cup liquid egg substitute
1¾ cups skim milk
¼ teaspoon seasoned salt
½ teaspoon garlic pepper

Preheat oven to 350°. Place half of bread cubes into greased 11 x 7 x 2-inch baking dish. Add spinach, basil and tomatoes. Top with half of cheese. Add remaining bread and sprinkle with remaining cheese. Beat together egg substitute, milk, seasoned salt and garlic pepper. Pour in dish. Cover and refrigerate overnight. Bake uncovered until puffy, about 45 minutes.

VEGETABLE CASSEROLE

Yields: 6 servings

2 tablespoons vegetable oil

2 large onions, peeled and sliced into
½-inch rings

½ cup barley, checked and rinsed

1 cup water

2 medium green peppers, cored,
seeded and sliced into ¼-inch
strips

2 large carrots, peeled and cut into
chunks

2 large tomatoes, peeled, seeded, cut
into chunks

1 small unpeeled zucchini, cut into
chunks

¾ pound green beans, tips removed,
cut into bite-size pieces

½ cup fresh or frozen peas

2 cups cauliflower florets

2 tablespoons lemon juice

3 tablespoons dry white wine

2 small cloves garlic, peeled and finely
minced

2 teaspoons salt

1½ teaspoons paprika

1½ teaspoons black pepper

⅓ cup fresh parsley, chopped

Preheat oven to 400°. Heat oil in skillet to medium and sauté onion rings 8-10 minutes, until translucent and slightly browned. Remove onions from pan and set aside. Combine barley and water in a 3-quart casserole greased with teaspoon of oil or sprayed with cooking spray. Mix all vegetables, except onions, and spread mixture over barley. Top with onions. Combine lemon juice, wine, garlic, spices and parsley and pour over casserole. Cover and bake 1½ hours if you plan to serve the casserole immediately or 1 hour if you plan to freeze it. If freezing, before serving, allow casserole to thaw almost completely, then bake 30-40 minutes.

Worth the Effort

At the
beginning of the Middle Ages, Arab and
possibly Jewish merchants brought the eggplant
with them from the east. Since that time it has been the most
versatile vegetable in the eastern Mediterranean.

Eggplant Parmesan

Yields: 8 servings

1 (2-pound) eggplant
1 tablespoon salt
1 cup flour
3 eggs, lightly beaten
1¾ cups seasoned bread crumbs

¾ cup oil divided into 3 parts
1½ cups shredded fresh mozzarella
    cheese
4 cups marinara sauce

Peel and cut eggplant in ¼ inch slices. Lightly salt slices on each side. Place a paper towel on top of a plate. Put one layer of eggplant covering paper towel. Cover eggplant with another paper towel. Continue layering eggplant and paper towels until you have used all the eggplant, finishing with a paper towel. Cover with a weighted plate for 30 minutes. (Eggplant has a lot of acid and this process helps take out some of that acid.)

Preheat oven to 325°. Heat ¼ cup oil in a large pan over medium-high heat.

Put flour, beaten eggs and bread crumbs in three separate bowls. Lightly coat the eggplant first with flour, then egg, and lastly bread crumbs. Fry eggplant in oil, being careful not to overcrowd in pan, 1½ minutes each side until lightly browned. Place fried eggplant on top of a paper towel to drain off some of the oil. Continue until all the eggplant is fried. You will need to change the oil twice while frying the eggplant.

Place fried eggplant in a 9 x 13-inch baking dish or foil pan. Cover with tomato sauce. Sprinkle with mozzarella cheese. Bake 25 minutes. Broil 2 minutes before serving.

Ricotta Spinach Pie

Yields: 6 servings

1 refrigerated pie crust (half 15-ounce package), room temperature
1 teaspoon all-purpose flour
3 tablespoons butter
1 medium onion, chopped
1 (10-ounce) package frozen chopped spinach, thawed and squeezed dry
½ teaspoon salt
½ teaspoon pepper
¼ teaspoon ground nutmeg
1 (15-ounce) container ricotta cheese
8 ounces mozzarella cheese, shredded
1 cup grated Parmesan cheese
3 large eggs, beaten

Preheat oven to 350°. Unfold pie crust. Press out fold lines; if crust cracks, wet fingers and push edges together to seal. Sprinkle flour over crust. Place crust floured side down in a 9 x 2-inch glass or ceramic pie dish. Fold edge under; crimp decoratively. Melt butter in a large, heavy skillet over medium heat. Add onion; sauté until tender, about 8 minutes. Mix in spinach, salt, pepper and nutmeg. Sauté until all liquid from spinach evaporates, about 3 minutes. Combine ricotta, mozzarella and Parmesan cheeses in a large bowl. Mix in eggs. Add spinach mixture; blend well. Spoon into pie crust. Bake until filling is set in center and brown on top, about 40 minutes. Let stand 10 minutes.

Spinach and Ricotta Stuffed Shells

Yields: 4 servings

12 ounces jumbo shells
1 tablespoon garlic powder
10 ounces frozen chopped spinach,
    thawed
½ cup milk
2 slices crustless white bread, crumbled

3 tablespoons olive oil
2¼ cups ricotta cheese
Pinch grated nutmeg
Salt and pepper, to taste
2 cups marinara sauce
¼ cup Parmesan cheese

Preheat oven to 325°. Cook pasta according to package instructions in salted water with garlic powder. Drain and rinse under cold water. Set aside.

Place spinach in a sieve and press out excess liquid. In a food processor, place milk, bread, and oil and process. Add spinach and ricotta, and season with nutmeg, salt, and pepper. Process briefly to combine.

Spread marinara sauce evenly over the bottom of a 13 x 9 x 2-inch dish.

Spoon spinach mixture into a pastry bag fitted with a large plain nozzle and fill pasta shells. (Or use a spoon.)

Arrange pasta shells over the sauce. Bake 15 minutes. Sprinkle Parmesan over shells. Broil until cheese browns.

VEGETABLE QUICHE

Yields: 6-8 servings

1 (9-inch) deep dish, frozen pie crust	3 eggs
1 medium onion, diced	¼ cup ricotta cheese
½ zucchini, sliced	½ cup milk
5-6 mushrooms, thickly sliced	½ teaspoon salt
½ red bell pepper, diced	⅛ teaspoon pepper
1 cup shredded mozzarella cheese or	¼ teaspoon oregano
Muenster cheese	½ teaspoon garlic powder

Preheat oven to 350°. Defrost pie crust. Sauté onion, zucchini, mushrooms and pepper until soft and most of liquid has evaporated. Drain remaining liquid. Sprinkle ¼ cup mozzarella and/or Muenster cheese on bottom of crust; top with vegetables. In a medium-size bowl, beat eggs; mix in ricotta cheese and ½ cup shredded cheese; add milk and stir in spices. Pour mixture over vegetables. Sprinkle remaining ¼ cup shredded cheese on top. Bake 1 hour or until top is gooey and brown.

This quiche freezes really well and is more "wet" than a classic quiche. Different vegetables will work, too. It makes excellent leftovers and reheats well.

VEGETARIAN CHILI

Yields: 16-20 cups

1 tablespoon olive oil
2 cups chopped onion
2 cups sliced fresh mushrooms
1½ cups diced carrots
2 cloves garlic, minced
2 cups red pepper, diced
2 (14½-ounce) cans tomatoes, diced
    and undrained
2 cups water
1 jalapeño pepper, seeded and chopped

1 tablespoon chili powder
1 teaspoon ground cumin
⅛ teaspoon black pepper
2 cups fresh broccoli florets
1 (16-ounce) can red kidney beans,
    undrained
½ cup plus 2 tablespoons plain yogurt,
    optional
⅓ cup shredded cheese, optional

Coat a large pot or Dutch oven with 1 tablespoon olive oil. Warm over medium-high flame. Add onions, mushrooms, carrots and garlic. Sauté until vegetables are just tender. Stir in red peppers, tomatoes, water, jalapeño pepper, chili powder, cumin and black pepper; stir well. Bring mixture to a boil. Cover, reduce heat and simmer 15 minutes. Stir in broccoli and kidney beans. Cover and simmer 20 minutes. Top each serving with 1 tablespoon yogurt and 1 tablespoon shredded cheese if desired.

GNOCCHI (POTATO DUMPLINGS)

Yields: 12 servings

3 pounds potatoes, peeled
2 egg yolks
½ teaspoon salt
⅛ teaspoon pepper

2 cups all-purpose flour
6 quarts water
½ cup canola oil

Boil whole potatoes until soft (about 45 minutes). While still warm, rice potatoes, using a ricer, into a bowl. Allow to cool.

Gently mix egg yolks, salt, and pepper into the cooled potatoes. Gradually mix in flour until a soft dough is formed. Do not over mix the dough or the gnocchi will be unpleasantly dense, mix just enough so dough is not sticky.

In a large saucepan, bring 6 quarts of water to a boil.

On a well-floured work surface, turn out the potato dough and divide into 6 equal parts. With the palms of both hands gently roll each part into a "rope" ¾-inch in diameter. Using a sharp knife cut each "rope" on an angle into ¾-inch-long pieces.

Prepare an ice bath, 6 cups of ice in 6 cups of water. Drop the dough pieces into boiling water and cook until they float (about 2 minutes). As gnocchi float to top of boiling water, remove them to the ice bath. After all gnocchi have been transferred, let sit several minutes in bath, then drain off ice and water. Toss with ½ cup canola oil and store covered in refrigerator until ready to serve (up to 48 hours).

For a simple pesto sauce, place 5 cups fresh basil, 8 cloves garlic, ½ cup pine nuts, and 1 teaspoon salt in food processor. As it purées, drizzle in ¾ cup olive oil.

You can also make green gnocchi by adding 14 ounces frozen leaf spinach, thawed and squeezed dry. Mix the spinach with the potato purée and continue.

Prepare Ahead of Time

Side Dishes and Vegetables

The manna tasted like the delicacies at a king's table, and would not assume the tastes of the vegetables of a poor man.

(Sefer Haparshiot, Parshas Bha'aloscha)

TASTY ROASTED POTATOES

Yields: 8-10 servings

1 teaspoon salt
1 teaspoon pepper
1 teaspoon paprika
1 teaspoon cumin

1 teaspoon garlic powder or fresh
    garlic, minced
1 teaspoon lemon peel
¼ cup vegetable oil
8-10 large redskin potatoes, unpeeled
    and quartered

Preheat oven to 400°.

Mix spices and lemon peel together and add to the oil. Toss potatoes in the mix and spread out in a single layer in a large baking pan. Bake uncovered 55-60 minutes or until brown and soft. Shake pan or mix potatoes a few times during cooking process to even the browning.

Holiday Favorite

SESAME NOODLES

Yields: 10-12 servings

PASTA
1 onion, thinly sliced
1 red pepper, thinly sliced
1 yellow pepper, thinly sliced

1 zucchini, thinly sliced
1 carrot, thinly sliced
2 pounds spaghetti

SAUCE
½ cup soy sauce
½ teaspoon ground ginger
½ cup vegetable oil

1 tablespoon sesame oil
¼ cup sugar

Pasta: Steam vegetables until tender, but still a little crunchy. Cook spaghetti according to package directions. Pour sauce over pasta and add vegetables. Serve chilled.

Sauce: Combine all ingredients. Cook in microwave 1 minute.

Crowd Pleaser

CRANBERRY AND PEAR CHUTNEY

Yields: 8 servings

1 (12-ounce) bag fresh or frozen
    cranberries
2 large (1 pound), firm-ripe Bartlett
    pears, peeled, cored and cut into
    ½-inch chunks
¾ cup chopped onion
¾ cup packed brown sugar

½ cup golden raisins
2 tablespoons red wine vinegar
2 tablespoons grated fresh ginger
¼ teaspoon salt
⅛ teaspoon ground cinnamon
⅛ teaspoon ground cloves

Place all ingredients in a 5-6-quart pot. Cover and bring to a boil. Simmer over low heat 20-25 minutes. Stir frequently, until mixture thickens. (It will thicken further when refrigerated.) Let cool and spoon into a storage container. Cover and refrigerate. Good for about 2 weeks when stored in the refrigerator.

TURNIP CASSEROLE

Yields: 6-8 servings

3 cups peeled, boiled turnips, mashed
5 tablespoons margarine
1 teaspoon sugar
1½ teaspoons salt

¼ teaspoon pepper
1¼ cups soft bread crumbs
2 eggs, beaten
2 tablespoons margarine, melted

Preheat oven to 350°. Combine turnips, margarine, sugar, salt, pepper, ¾ cup bread crumbs and eggs. Mix well. Pour into a buttered 1-quart casserole dish and top with remaining bread crumbs mixed with 2 tablespoons melted margarine. Bake 35 minutes or until brown.

BROWN AND WILD RICE SALAD

Yields: 10-12 servings

DRESSING

⅓ cup vegetable oil
½ cup white vinegar
1 tablespoon sugar
2 teaspoons salt
1 teaspoon celery salt

½ teaspoon white pepper
½ teaspoon paprika
1 garlic clove, minced
½ teaspoon dry mustard

SALAD

8 cups cooked brown and wild rice mix
1 (14-ounce) jar hearts of palm, drained
     and sliced
1 (10-ounce) package frozen peas

1 red bell pepper, chopped
4 stems green onion, chopped
1 (6-ounce) package slivered almonds,
     toasted

Dressing: Combine all ingredients in lidded jar and shake well. Refrigerate until ready to use.

Salad: Mix rice and hearts of palm with peas, red peppers and green onions. Toss well with half of dressing. Cover and chill. Just before serving, add remaining dressing and toss again. Top with almonds.

Crowd Pleaser

GARLIC BROCCOLI PASTA

Yields: 4 servings

6 ounces rigatoni or large tube pasta, uncooked
2 cups fresh broccoli florets
3 garlic cloves, minced

4½ teaspoons olive oil
¼ cup shredded Parmesan cheese
½ teaspoon salt
⅛ teaspoon white pepper

Cook pasta according to package directions. During last two minutes of cooking add broccoli to pasta. Drain pasta and broccoli. In a saucepan, sauté garlic in oil until tender. Add pasta and broccoli. Toss to coat. Add Parmesan cheese, salt and pepper and toss again.

ASPARAGUS CASSEROLE

Yields: 8-10 servings

2 cups cream of mushroom soup
¼ cup chopped onion
¼ cup milk
2-4 tablespoons butter
8 ounces cream cheese, room temperature

1-1½ pounds fresh asparagus, woody stems removed
4 hard boiled eggs, sliced or diced
⅓ cup seasoned bread crumbs

Preheat oven to 350°. Mix soup, onions, milk, butter and cream cheese. Heat slowly until completely blended. Layer asparagus, sliced eggs and cream mixture twice in a 13 x 9 x 2-inch pan. Sprinkle with bread crumbs. Bake 40 minutes. Let sit 10-15 minutes before serving.

APPLE CRANBERRY BAKE

Yields: 6-8 servings

½ cup white sugar
½ cup brown sugar
1 cup uncooked quick oatmeal
3 tablespoons flour
1 teaspoon cinnamon

1½ cups fresh cranberries
3 medium apples, peeled, cored and
   diced
1 cup chopped pecans, optional
½ cup margarine

Preheat oven to 350°. Combine white sugar, brown sugar, oatmeal, flour and cinnamon. Add fruit and nuts. Mix well by hand. Spread in deep casserole dish. Dot with margarine. Bake 30 minutes or until golden.

Good for Thanksgiving. Consider buying cranberries at Thanksgiving, when there is an abundance of them, and freezing them for use year-round. Fresh cranberries make this recipe, so do not skimp and use canned cranberries. It can also be used as a dessert and served with ice cream.

Kid's Pick

RAISIN CURRIED COUSCOUS

Yields: 6 servings

3 cups water
1½ cups couscous, uncooked
4 tablespoons olive oil

1 cup raisins
1 teaspoon curry powder

Bring water to a boil in a small saucepan. Add couscous and let stand 5 minutes. Pour olive oil in a sauté pan over medium-low heat, add raisins and curry. Cook until the raisins are plumped. Stir in couscous, combine and serve immediately.

SQUASH FLAN

Yields: 8 servings

3 eggs
½ cup flour
½ cup sugar
4 tablespoons margarine, melted
1 cup non-dairy creamer

1 cup water
1 (12-ounce) package frozen squash, defrosted
Nutmeg or cinnamon to taste, optional

Preheat oven to 350°. Beat eggs, flour, sugar, margarine, creamer and water. Mix in squash. Put in greased 8-inch square pan. Sprinkle with nutmeg or cinnamon. Bake 1 hour.

For a twist in flavor use vanilla soy milk in place of non-dairy creamer.

_____

Kid's Pick

_____

Honey Almond Sweet Potatoes

Yields: 10-12 servings

8 sweet potatoes, peeled
½ cup honey
¼ cup orange marmalade
2 tablespoons water

½ teaspoon salt
¼ cup margarine
½ cup slivered almonds, blanched

Preheat oven to 325°. Cook sweet potatoes until partially done. Cut in half lengthwise. Place in greased pan. Combine honey, marmalade, water and salt. Bring to a boil. Simmer 5 minutes. Pour over potatoes. Melt margarine. Add almonds and toast over low heat for a few minutes. Sprinkle over potatoes. Bake 30 minutes. Baste while baking.

Chef's Choice

HIMALAYAN RED RICE

Yields: 10 servings

2½ cups vegetable stock
1 cup Himalayan red rice, uncooked
½ cup chopped green onions
1 cinnamon stick
1 whole star anise, cut into slices

1 cup chopped Granny Smith apple
   with skin
1 tablespoon toasted, crushed almonds
⅛ teaspoon freshly ground pepper
¼ teaspoon sea salt

In a medium saucepan, combine vegetable stock, rice, green onions, cinnamon stick and star anise. Bring to a boil and reduce heat to a simmer and cover. Simmer 40 minutes, until rice is starting to soften.

Remove from heat and mix in apple, almond, pepper and salt. Cover again and let rice steep 5 more minutes. Fluff with a fork, remove cinnamon stick and serve.

CHINESE VEGETABLES

Yields: 8-10 servings

1 medium head Chinese cabbage
2 celery stalks
3 green onions
2 tablespoons vegetable oil
¼ cup water

1 (8-ounce) package frozen snow peas, thawed
3 tablespoons soy sauce
2 pimientos, chopped
Salt to taste, optional

Slice cabbage, celery and onions diagonally. Put vegetables in a large saucepan and add oil and water. Cover and steam 5 minutes. Add snow peas and soy sauce. Cover and steam a few minutes longer, or until vegetables are tender, but still crisp. Add pimientos and salt to taste.

For added flavor, substitute chopped red peppers for pimientos.

When potatoes were introduced from the New World, the Ashkenazi Jews enthusiastically incorporated them into their cuisine, creating latkes and kugels, soups and dumplings.

CRISPY POTATO LATKES

Yields: 9 extra-large latkes

2 pounds baking potatoes, peeled and shredded
1 medium onion, coarsely grated
6 tablespoons all-purpose flour

2 large eggs, beaten
½ cup vegetable oil
Salt and pepper, to taste

In a bowl, mix potatoes, onion, flour and eggs. Season well with salt and pepper. In a skillet, heat ¼ cup oil until shimmering. Drop about ¼ cup latke mixture into skillet and spread slightly. Cook over moderately high heat until brown on the bottom, about 7 minutes. Turn and cook until brown, about 4 minutes. Transfer to paper towel. Continue cooking until latke mixture is gone. Season with salt and pepper and serve hot.

Holiday Favorite

SWEET CARROTS

Yields: 4-6 servings

**5 carrots, peeled, sliced ¼-inch thick
(or use 1 pound baby carrots)**
2 teaspoons sugar
½ teaspoon cinnamon
½ stick unsalted margarine

½ tablespoon orange juice
Salt and pepper to taste
10 dried apricots, sliced
⅓ cup sliced toasted almonds, optional

Place carrots in a saucepan, cover with cold water and bring to a boil over medium heat. Reduce heat and simmer 10 minutes. Rinse under cold water and drain. In a small bowl, stir together sugar and cinnamon. Melt margarine in skillet. Stir in carrots and orange juice. Sprinkle with sugar-cinnamon mixture and cook until carrots are glazed and sauce is slightly thickened, about 5 minutes. Season with salt and pepper. Stir in apricots and almonds and cook just until heated through.

Penne with Mushrooms, Tomatoes and Basil

Yields: 4 servings

¾ pound penne pasta
6 tablespoons olive oil
1 small onion, chopped
6 large garlic cloves, chopped
¾ pound mushrooms, thickly sliced
2 teaspoons chopped fresh rosemary or
    1½ teaspoons dried

½ cup chopped fresh basil
⅔ cup dry white wine
1 (14½- to 16-ounce) can diced
    tomatoes
1 cup pareve chicken broth
Grated Parmesan cheese

Cook pasta according to package directions. While pasta is cooking, heat oil in a heavy large pot over medium-high heat. Add onion and garlic and sauté 1 minute. Add mushrooms, rosemary and ¼ cup basil. Sauté until onion and mushrooms are tender, about 8 minutes. Add wine. Boil until most of wine evaporates, about 3 minutes. Add tomatoes with their juices, and broth. Boil until sauce thickens slightly, stirring occasionally, about 5 minutes. Add penne and remaining ¼ cup basil to pot. Toss pasta with sauce until well coated and heated through. Season to taste with salt and pepper. Serve with Parmesan cheese on side.

MEATY POTATO KNISHES

Yields: 4-6 servings

4 large potatoes, boiled and mashed
2 eggs, beaten separately
Salt and pepper to taste
1 tablespoon margarine
Matzo meal, as needed

Leftover cooked roast or ground
    beef, about 1 pound, ground if
    necessary
1 medium onion, sliced and sautéed
Paprika to taste
Cinnamon, optional

Preheat oven to 350°. Combine mashed potatoes with 1 beaten egg, salt, pepper and margarine. If loose, add enough matzo meal so that mixture can be handled. Combine ground-up meat with sautéed onion. Add remaining egg and season to taste. Oil hands and take scoop of potatoes. Shape gently into a round and make a hole in the center. Put 1 tablespoon meat mixture in center and cover with potato mixture. Place knishes in greased 13 x 9 x 2-inch baking dish. Sprinkle with paprika and bake until brown.

Cinnamon added to meat spices this dish up.

GREEN BEAN BUNDLES

Yields: 8 servings

1 pound fresh green beans, trimmed
2 yellow summer squash, cut into
    1½-inch slices
1 garlic clove, minced

¼ teaspoon dried tarragon, crushed
4 teaspoons olive oil
¼ teaspoon salt
¼ teaspoon coarsely ground pepper

Arrange green beans in 8 bundles. Hollow squash slices to within ¼ inch of edges. Insert each bundle of green beans into a squash ring. Place bundles in a steamer basket. Put basket in a saucepan over 1 inch of water, bring to a boil. Cover, steam 8-10 minutes or until tender, but still crisp. In a small nonstick skillet, sauté garlic and tarragon in oil 1 minute. Arrange bundles on serving platter, drizzle with garlic mixture, sprinkle with salt and pepper.

This dish is pretty enough to serve as a centerpiece and is a tasty addition to any meal.

FRESH HORSERADISH

Yields: 12 servings

2 medium beets, about 10 ounces
1 (4-ounce) piece horseradish, peeled
    (make sure it is firm, not mushy or
    overly wrinkled)

2 teaspoons salt
1 teaspoon sugar

Scrub beets, trim stems to ½ inch. Place in a medium saucepan, add water to cover by 1 inch. Bring to a boil over high heat, cook at gentle boil until beets are tender when pierced with small, sharp knife, about 45 minutes. Remove from heat, drain, set beets aside until cool enough to handle. Grate horseradish on the medium-size holes of a box grater, add vinegar, salt and sugar, stir well. Peel beets, grate on the medium-size holes of the box grater. Add to horseradish mixture and stir well to combine. Keep covered to preserve flavor, and refrigerate until needed.

Very easy, very good and very pretty. It keeps well so make it several days before the Seder and feel like you've gotten started early.

Prepare Ahead of Time

Barley Casserole

Yields: 6-8 servings

4 tablespoons unsalted margarine
2 medium onions, finely chopped
½ pound mushrooms, sliced
1½ cups uncooked barley

3 cups prepared pareve chicken
   bouillon
Pepper to taste

Preheat oven to 350°. On medium heat, melt margarine in large frying pan. Add onions and sauté 2 minutes. Add mushrooms and continue to sauté until soft. Add barley and cook until lightly browned. Add bouillon, pepper and stir. Bring to boil, cover. Bake 45 minutes to 1 hour.

Best when served hot.

Baked Squash

Yields: 12-14 servings

3 pounds yellow squash
½ cup chopped onions
1½ cups cornflake crumbs
2 eggs

½ cup margarine
1 teaspoon sugar
1 teaspoon salt
½ teaspoon black pepper

Preheat oven to 375°. Peel and slice squash. In a medium size saucepan, cook squash until tender in about 1-inch of water. Drain well and mash. Add onions, ½ cup cornflakes, pepper, eggs, ¼ cup margarine, sugar, salt and pepper. Melt remaining ¼ cup of margarine. Pour mixture into a 13 x 9 x 2-inch baking dish and pour melted margarine over top. Sprinkle with remaining cornflake crumbs. Bake 1 hour.

Delicious. This recipe is also good if you don't want to mash the squash.

BAKED SPINACH RISOTTO

Yields: 6-8 servings

3 cups fresh chopped spinach
1 tablespoon olive oil
1 green bell pepper, chopped
1 medium onion, chopped
2 garlic cloves, minced

1 cup uncooked Arborio rice
1 (14½-ounce) can pareve chicken
    broth
½ cup grated Parmesan cheese
1 teaspoon salt

Preheat oven to 400°. Grease 1½-quart casserole dish. Heat oil in a 10-inch skillet over medium heat. Add green bell pepper, onion, and garlic, cook 5 minutes. Add rice, stir to coat well. Stir in spinach, broth, ¼ cup cheese and salt. Spoon mixture into a prepared baking dish. Sprinkle with remaining ¼ cup cheese. Bake 35-40 minutes until rice is tender.

CASTILIAN POTATO CASSEROLE

Yields: 8 servings

6 medium baking potatoes, peeled and
    quartered
½ cup plain yogurt
2 tablespoons butter
¼-½ teaspoon salt
⅛ teaspoon ground red pepper

2 eggs, beaten
¾ cup herbed feta cheese
¼ cup water
1 (20-ounce) package pre-washed
    spinach
¼ teaspoon paprika

Preheat oven to 425°. Place potatoes in a large saucepan with a small amount of boiling water; cover and cook 25 minutes or until tender. Drain and mash. Add yogurt, butter, salt, and red pepper; beat just until combined. Add eggs; beat with an electric mixer on low speed 1 minute or until fluffy. Fold in ½ cup feta cheese. In a 12-inch skillet, bring the water to a boil and add spinach. Toss spinach about 1 minute or until slightly wilted; drain. Press out excess liquid and coarsely chop. Spread half potato mixture into a lightly greased 13 x 9 x 2-inch baking dish. Layer spinach on top and sprinkle with remaining feta cheese. Spread remaining potato mixture on top of this and sprinkle with paprika. Bake, uncovered, 15 minutes or until top is lightly browned.

At the Moroccan table, presentation and hospitality are almost as important as the food itself. The serving pieces are so beautiful that there is no need for garnishes.

MOROCCAN-STYLE SQUASH STEW

Yields: 10-12 servings

1½ pounds butternut squash, peeled, seeded and medium diced

3 tablespoons vegetable oil

1 teaspoon ground coriander

2 teaspoons ground cumin

½ teaspoon sweet paprika

3 medium onions, finely chopped

3 garlic cloves, minced

2 cups prepared vegetable broth

1 (14-ounce) can petite diced tomatoes with juice

1 carrot, finely chopped

1 parsnip, finely chopped

¼ teaspoon cayenne pepper

¼ teaspoon cinnamon

Kosher salt, to taste

1 (7½-ounce) can chickpeas, drained

¼ cup cilantro, coarsely chopped

1 tablespoon fresh lemon juice

Preheat oven to 350°. On a large baking sheet, toss the squash with 2 tablespoons oil. Roast 15 minutes. In a large saucepan, toast the coriander, cumin, and paprika over moderate heat, stirring 2 minutes. Transfer to a small bowl to cool. Heat remaining 1 tablespoon oil in the pan. Add onions and garlic and cook over medium heat for 10 minutes. Add squash, broth, tomatoes with juice, carrots, parsnips, cayenne, cinnamon, and toasted spices. Season with salt and bring to a boil. Cover and simmer over low heat 10 minutes. Uncover, add chickpeas, and simmer 10 minutes longer. Stir in cilantro and lemon juice. Serve.

Even better the next day.

To turn this into a wonderful chicken dish, prepare as instructed, pour over 12 boneless, skinless chicken thighs, cover and bake 1 hour at 325°.

Chef's Choice

FOURTEEN-LAYER RIBBON MOLD

Yields: 24 servings

7 (3-ounce) packages varied flavors
    gelatin
1 pint sour cream

7 cups boiling water
    (1 cup per package for each layer)
Cooking spray

Dissolve 1 package gelatin in 1 cup boiling water. Pour ⅔ cup into a deep decorative serving dish or mold that has been sprayed with cooking spray. Refrigerate until gelatin is set. Mix ⅓ cup sour cream with remaining ⅓ cup prepared gelatin. Allow new layer of gelatin to cool slightly. Spoon over refrigerated gelatin. Continue this process until all gelatin packages and remaining sour cream are used. When complete and gelatin and sour cream layers have jelled, cut into squares and serve.

You can put the gelatin in the freezer for about 10 minutes to speed up gel time between layers.

Worth the Effort

RATATOUILLE IN PHYLLO

Yields: 6-8 servings

RATATOUILLE
1 small eggplant, peeled and cut into
    ½-inch cubes
1 large onion, chopped
3 tablespoons oil
1 green pepper, chopped
2 stalks celery, chopped
2 carrots, chopped
¼ pound mushrooms, sliced
1 garlic clove, crushed
1 teaspoon fresh basil
½ cup bread crumbs
½ cup fresh parsley
Salt and pepper to taste

DOUGH
6 sheets phyllo dough
3 tablespoons oil
¼ pound feta cheese

SAUCE
1 large onion, chopped
2 tablespoons oil
2 garlic cloves, crushed
1 (28-ounce) can whole peeled
    tomatoes, drained
3 tablespoons tomato paste
¾ cup pareve chicken bouillon
½ teaspoon cinnamon
1 teaspoon salt
Pepper to taste

Preheat oven to 375°.

Ratatouille: Place ⅓ of eggplant in a colander, salt heavily. Repeat 2 more times. Cover with inverted plate and weigh down with heavy object. Let stand 30 minutes. Rinse well and set aside. Sauté onion in oil 5 minutes. Add green pepper, celery and carrots and sauté 5 minutes. Add mushrooms, garlic and basil and sauté 3 minutes. Add eggplant. Toss well to incorporate. Cover and cook 10 minutes, stirring frequently. Add bread crumbs, parsley, salt and pepper. Mix well and set aside to cool.

Dough: Lay one sheet of phyllo on a clean dish towel. Brush with oil. Lay another sheet on top. Brush again with oil. Repeat until all phyllo is used. Spread ratatouille on dough leaving a 1-inch margin. Sprinkle feta cheese on the ratatouille. Turn in ends and roll into a loaf. Lay seam side down on a large baking pan. Brush with oil. With a small, sharp knife, cut slits in loaf*. Bake 35-40 minutes or until brown.

Sauce: Prepare bouillon according to package directions. Sauté onion in oil until limp. Add garlic and cook 2-3 minutes. Drain tomatoes, remove seeds and chop pulp. Add pulp to onions, along with tomato paste, chicken broth, cinnamon, salt and pepper. Simmer 30 minutes. Pour sauce over loaf before serving.

Slits should represent the size of serving pieces; makes it easier to cut after done.

Desserts

The people roamed about and
gathered it…and made it into cakes and its
taste was like the taste of an oil cake.

(Parshas Bha'aloscha 11,8)

And the House of Israel
called it manna…and it tasted like
a cake fried in honey.

(Parshas B'shalach 16,31)

Just a Reminder…
green = pareve   red = meat   blue = dairy

BOURBON SLUSH

Yields: 1½ quarts

1 or 2 tea bags
1 cup boiling water
1 cup sugar
2½ cups water

½ cup bourbon
⅔ cup frozen orange juice concentrate, thawed or ⅓ cup frozen lemonade concentrate, thawed

Steep tea bag(s) in 1 cup boiling water 2-5 minutes. Remove tea bags. Stir in sugar. Add remaining ingredients. Mix until sugar is dissolved. Pour into freezer container and freeze until firm. Remove 10 minutes before serving. Spoon into glasses. Store until ready to serve and serve slightly defrosted like a slush.

A must for your next cookout! It's really "yum."

COFFEE GRANITA

Yields: 6-8 servings

2 cups prepared black coffee, lukewarm
½ cup sugar
2 tablespoons liqueur, coffee or
    chocolate flavored

1 teaspoon lemon zest
Whipped cream, optional

Combine all ingredients until sugar melts. Pour into a 13 x 9 x 2-inch pan, glass or metal, and place in freezer 30-45 minutes. With fork, break up any ice crystals that have formed around the edges and stir mixture briefly, return to freezer. Repeat every 30 minutes or so for 2-3 hours until mixture is dry and fluffy. Serve in chilled bowls or goblets, adding whipped cream if desired.

HELLO DOLLIES

Yields: 1 dozen

1 stick butter, melted
1 cup graham cracker crumbs
1 (6-ounce) package chocolate chips
1 (6-ounce) package butterscotch bits

1 cup pecans, chopped
1 cup unsweetened condensed milk
1 cup shredded, sweetened coconut, optional

Preheat oven to 350°. Pour melted butter into 13 x 9 x 2-inch pan. Layer the remaining ingredients, one at a time, in the above order. Bake 25 minutes. Cut while warm. Leave in pan until cooled.

You can also use margarine or any kind of fat-free or calorie-free butter/margarine and they still taste great.

EASY FUDGE

Yields: 64 (1-inch) squares

1 box confectioners' sugar
¼ cup milk
¼ cup cocoa

1 teaspoon vanilla
1 stick butter
1 cup walnuts, chopped

Mix together sugar, milk, cocoa and vanilla and place butter on top. Microwave on high 2 minutes, rotating dish after 1 minute. Mix. Add chopped walnuts. Mix again. Pour into wax paper-lined 8-inch square pan. Refrigerate until hard, 1-2 hours. Cut into squares.

CARAMEL BARS

Yields: 28 bars

⅔ cup margarine
1½ cups flour
2 cups brown sugar, packed
2 teaspoons baking powder

3 eggs, well beaten
¼ teaspoon salt
1 teaspoon vanilla
¾ cup walnuts, chopped

Preheat oven to 350°. Melt margarine in a saucepan. Remove from heat and add remaining ingredients. Mix thoroughly. Spread batter in a buttered and floured 13 x 9 x 2-inch pan. Bake 30-35 minutes. Cool before cutting into squares.

CHOCOLATE CHIP PECAN PIE

Yields: 8-10 servings

1 cup corn syrup
2 eggs, beaten
1 cup sugar
2 tablespoons margarine

1 teaspoon vanilla
1½ cups whole pecans
1 cup chocolate chips
1 (9-inch) pie crust

Preheat oven to 425°. Combine corn syrup, eggs, sugar, margarine and vanilla. Add pecans and chocolate chips. Mix well. Pour into pie shell. Bake 15 minutes. Reduce temperature to 350° for additional 4-5 minutes. Cool to room temperature before serving.

Delicious and gooey, all that a pecan pie should be!

OLD-FASHIONED POUND CAKE

Yields: 12 servings

3 cups flour
3 teaspoons baking powder
3 cups sugar
5 large eggs

¾ cup oil
2 teaspoons vanilla
¾ cup pareve margarine
1 cup non-dairy creamer

Preheat oven to 350°. Combine all ingredients and mix with hand mixer on high for 5 minutes. Pour into greased, deep 9-inch Bundt pan. Bake 1-1½ hours or until toothpick comes out clean.

FRUIT COBBLER

Yields: 10-12 servings

½ cup margarine
1 cup flour
1 cup sugar
1 cup soy milk

2 teaspoons baking powder
2-4 cups of any fruit in season, cut and sweetened to taste

Preheat oven to 350°. Melt margarine in casserole dish in oven. Mix together flour, sugar, soy milk and baking powder. Pour batter on top of margarine but do not stir in. Add fruit on top of batter. Leave edge of batter all around fruit. Bake 45 minutes to 1 hour until golden brown and fruit is bubbly.

Quick n Easy

RASPBERRY CHOCOLATE SAUCE

Yields: 1½ cups

1 (10-ounce) package frozen
    raspberries in syrup, thawed
4 ounces sweet chocolate, cut into
    pieces

3 tablespoons unsweetened cocoa
    powder
¼ cup confectioners' sugar
2 tablespoons unsalted butter, softened

In a small saucepan bring raspberries to a boil in their syrup. In a food processor, chop the chocolate coarsely and, with the motor running, add boiled raspberries, blending until smooth. Add cocoa powder, sugar and butter, blend sauce until combined well. Serve as a topping for ice cream.

Good on pound cake, cheese cake, angel food cake, and ice cream.

EASY BLUEBERRY SWIRL CHEESECAKE

Yields: 8 servings

2 (8-ounce) packages cream cheese,
    softened
½ cup sugar
¼ teaspoon vanilla

2 eggs
1 prepared (9-inch) graham cracker pie
    crust
1 (21-ounce) can blueberry pie filling

Preheat oven to 350°. Mix cream cheese, sugar and vanilla until smooth and creamy. Add eggs and mix well. Pour into pie crust. Spoon in ⅓ pie filling and swirl with a toothpick. Bake 40 minutes or until set. Cool and serve at room temperature with remaining filling as topping.

Other fruit fillings can be substituted.

Desserts

PLUM TORTE

Yields: 16 servings

TORTE
½ cup unsalted margarine
¾ cup sugar
1 cup unbleached flour, sifted
1 teaspoon baking powder

Pinch salt
2 eggs
Approx. 24 halves purple plums, pitted
    (less if using regular size plums)

TOPPING
1 tablespoon sugar
1 teaspoon lemon juice

1 teaspoon cinnamon

Preheat oven to 350°. Cream margarine and sugar in a bowl. Add flour, baking powder, salt and eggs. Beat well. Spoon batter into an 8-inch, 9-inch or 10-inch greased springform pan. Place plum halves, skin side up, on top of the batter. Sprinkle lightly with sugar, lemon juice and cinnamon. Bake one hour. Remove and cool; refrigerate or freeze if desired.

BEST-EVER GINGERSNAPS

Yields: 5-6 dozen

1 cup sugar
2 cups flour
½ teaspoon salt
1 teaspoon baking soda
1 teaspoon cinnamon
1 teaspoon ground ginger

½ teaspoon ground cloves
¾ cup shortening
¼ cup molasses
1 egg, slightly beaten
Sugar for coating

Preheat oven to 350° Combine sugar, flour, salt, baking soda and spices. Stir lightly. Cut in shortening to resemble coarse crumbs. Stir in molasses and egg. Shape dough into 1-inch balls and roll in sugar. Place on ungreased baking sheets. Bake 10 minutes. Remove immediately.

PEANUT BUTTER-CHOCOLATE CRISPY TREATS

Yields: 12-15 squares

¼ cup honey
½ cup corn syrup
1½ cups creamy peanut butter, divided
⅔ cup chocolate chips

4 cups crisped rice cereal
1 (12-ounce) bag white chocolate chips
Additional chocolate for drizzling

Melt honey, corn syrup, 1 cup peanut butter and chocolate chips. Add cereal. Pour into greased 13 x 9 x 2-inch pan and flatten. Melt white chocolate and ½ cup peanut butter. Pour over crispies mixture. Melt a little more chocolate and drizzle over white chocolate. Use a knife to swirl. Let cool.

Kids' Pick

Rum Cake

Yields: 12-16 servings

CAKE
1 box yellow cake mix
4 eggs
1 package instant vanilla pudding

½ cup water
½ cup oil
½ cup rum

GLAZE
1 stick margarine
¼ cup water

1 cup sugar
½ cup rum

Cake: Mix ingredients and bake according to cake box directions. When cake cools, poke holes into it.

Glaze: Boil margarine, water and sugar 5 minutes, stirring constantly. Add rum. Dribble glaze over cake until it is absorbed.

Try it with bourbon for a southern treat.

Pareve Ice Cream

Yields: 8-10 servings

4 eggs, separated
½ cup sugar
16 ounces pareve whip

2 teaspoons flavoring
Food coloring

In a small mixing bowl, beat egg whites and add sugar. In a larger mixing bowl, whip pareve whip. Add flavoring and food color. Fold in egg yolks and egg white mixture. Freeze.

Feel free to play around with different instant pudding mixes or fruits for flavoring. Our favorites are chocolate, mint chocolate chip and strawberry.

ICE CREAM CAKE

Yields: 10 servings

CAKE
2 quarts ice cream
1 (¾-pound) package soft batch cookies

Chocolate-covered toffee candy bar crumbles

FUDGE
2 squares unsweetened baker's chocolate
2 tablespoons butter

1 small can evaporated milk
1½ cups confectioners' sugar, sifted

Cake: Grease springform pan. Line bottom and sides of pan with cookies. Add 1 quart softened ice cream. Place cookies on top of this layer. Spoon 4 large spoons of fudge on top. Freeze. Once frozen, add 1 quart softened ice cream. Sprinkle candy bar crumbles on top. Spoon on more fudge. Freeze.

Fudge: Melt chocolate and butter in double boiler, then add milk and sugar. Stir until thick.

Prepare Ahead of Time

GRANDMA'S OATMEAL COOKIES

Yields: 5 dozen

1 cup shortening
½ cup margarine
1 cup sugar
1 cup brown sugar
2 eggs, beaten
1 teaspoon vanilla

1½ cups flour
1 teaspoon baking powder
1 teaspoon baking soda
2½ cups old-fashioned oats
1 cup raisins

Preheat oven to 350°. Mix shortening, margarine and sugars. Add eggs and vanilla and beat well. Sift flour with baking powder and baking soda. Add to mixture. Stir in oatmeal and raisins. Drop by teaspoonfuls onto greased cookie sheet. Bake 10 minutes.

MARBLE SQUARES

Yields: 2 dozen

½ cup margarine, softened
¼ cup plus 2 tablespoons sugar
¼ cup plus 2 tablespoons brown sugar
½ teaspoon vanilla
1 egg

1 cup flour
½ teaspoon baking soda
½ cup walnuts, coarsely chopped
1 cup semi-sweet chocolate chips

Preheat oven to 350°. Grease 13 x 9 x 2-inch pan. Mix margarine, sugars and vanilla. Beat in egg. Blend in flour and baking soda. Mix in nuts. Spread in greased pan. Sprinkle with chocolate chips. Bake 1 minute. Remove pan from oven and swirl chips into dough. Return to oven and bake 14 more minutes.

RAZZLE-APPLE STREUSEL BARS

Yields: 2 dozen

CRUST AND STREUSEL

2 cups oats (quick or old-fashioned, uncooked)

2½ cups flour

1¼ cups sugar

2 teaspoons baking powder

1 cup margarine, melted

FILLING

3 medium apples, thinly sliced, about 3 cups

2 tablespoons flour

1 (12-ounce) jar raspberry or apricot preserves

Preheat oven to 375°.

Crust and Streusel: Combine oats, flour, sugar and baking powder, mix well. Add margarine and mix until moistened. Reserve 2 cups of mixture. Press remaining mixture into bottom of greased 13 x 9 x 2-inch pan. Bake 15 minutes.

Filling: Combine apples and flour in a large bowl, stir in preserves. Spread on crust to within half inch of edge. Sprinkle with reserved crust mixture; press lightly. Bake 30-35 minutes.

FROZEN CHOCOLATE PEANUT BUTTER PIE

Yields: 10-12 servings

¾ package tea biscuits
½ cup margarine, melted
3 tablespoons brown sugar
5 eggs
½ cup sugar

1 cup pareve whip
1 teaspoon vanilla
½ cup chocolate syrup
½ cup light corn syrup
½ cup crunchy peanut butter

Preheat oven to 350°. Crush tea biscuits in a food processor. Mix crushed biscuits, melted margarine and brown sugar. Spread mixture into a 13 x 9-inch pan and bake 10 minutes. Cool completely. Beat eggs and sugar, add whip and vanilla and mix until blended. Pour mixture on crust and freeze. Mix chocolate syrup, corn syrup and peanut butter. Pour on top of frozen layers and refreeze. Serve frozen.

Prepare ahead of time

UNBELIEVABLE COOKIES

Yields: 112 Cookies

2 cups butter
2 cups sugar
2 cups brown sugar
4 eggs
2 tablespoons vanilla
4 cups flour
3 cups dry oatmeal (blend to a fine
    powder in blender)

1 teaspoon salt
1 teaspoon baking powder
2 teaspoons baking soda
1 (24-ounce) bag chocolate chips
1 (8-ounce) chocolate bar, grated
3 cups pecans, chopped

Preheat oven to 375°. Cream butter with sugars. Add eggs and vanilla. Mix together dry ingredients and add. Add chocolate and nuts. Roll into balls; place 2 inches apart on greased cookie sheet. Bake 6 minutes.

Desserts

MOIST CHOCOLATE CAKE

Yields: 10-12 servings

CAKE
2 cups sugar
2 cups flour
1 cup cocoa
1 teaspoon baking soda
1 teaspoon baking powder
1 teaspoon salt

1 cup vegetable oil
2 eggs
1 cup soy milk
1 teaspoon vanilla
1 cup boiling water

ICING
6 tablespoons oil
⅔ cup packed brown sugar
5 tablespoons soy milk

1½ cups confectioners' sugar, sifted
1 teaspoon vanilla

Cake: Preheat oven to 375°. Grease 10-inch Bundt pan. Mix all dry ingredients. Add all liquids except boiling water. Mix well, then add boiling water. Pour into Bundt pan, bake 45-50 minutes. Allow to cool before removing from pan.

Icing: Combine ingredients for the icing and mix until smooth. Pour on top of cake, allowing it to drizzle down. Sprinkle sides with confectioners' sugar.

LEMON-BLUEBERRY TRIFLE

Yields: 12-16 servings

1 lemon pound cake, cut into
    ½-inch slices
1 (3¾-ounce) package instant vanilla
    pudding mix
1 cup heavy cream
1 cup milk

½ teaspoon almond extract
Dry sherry
1 (21-ounce) can blueberry pie filling
2 ounces sliced almonds, toasted
1 cup heavy cream, whipped

Prepare pudding according to package directions using heavy cream and milk. Stir in almond extract. Cover and refrigerate about 5 minutes. Arrange half of cake slices in bottom of 13 x 9 x 2-inch baking dish. Sprinkle lightly with sherry. Spread half of pudding evenly over cake. Top with half of pie filling. Sprinkle with half of almonds. Repeat layering. Cover and chill at least 1 hour. Top with whipped cream.

TOFFEE TRIFLE

Yields: 12 servings

1 pound prepared pound cake
¾ cup coffee liqueur
3 cups half-and-half
1 (5⅜-ounce) package instant vanilla
    pudding mix
2 tablespoons instant coffee

2 cups heavy cream
2 tablespoons sugar
1 teaspoon vanilla
¼ pound chocolate-covered toffee
    candy bar pieces

Cut pound cake into cubes, cover with coffee liqueur and let stand. Mix half-and-half into instant pudding and whisk 2 minutes. Let sit 5 minutes. Add pudding mixture to pound cake. Add coffee to heavy cream and dissolve. Whip until firm. Add sugar and vanilla; whip another minute. Layer cake on bottom of trifle bowl, followed by whipped cream, then chocolate-covered toffee candy bar pieces. Repeat. If there is any whipped cream remaining, decorate top of trifle using pastry tube.

BLACK FOREST TRIFLE

Yields: 12 servings

1 (5⅜-ounce) package instant chocolate
    pudding mix
1 prepared jelly roll or chocolate pound
    cake, sliced
¼ cup liqueur

1 (25-ounce) can cherry pie filling or
    2 (16-ounce) cans pitted Bing
    cherries, well drained
1 cup heavy cream
¼ cup slivered almonds, toasted
1 ounce semi-sweet chocolate, shaved
Maraschino cherries with stems

Prepare chocolate pudding according to package directions. Set aside. Arrange slices of cake on bottom and sides of an attractive glass bowl. Sprinkle generously with all but 2 tablespoons of liqueur. Pour pudding on top of cake slices. Spread cherry filling over pudding. Refrigerate several hours or overnight. Whip cream, adding two tablespoons liqueur while whipping. Spoon or pipe whipped cream over cherry filling. Decorate with almonds, shaved chocolate and Maraschino cherries.

This dessert can be made early the day it will be served and refrigerated.

CHOCOLATE ÉCLAIR CAKE

Yields: 12-16 servings

1 box graham crackers, whole

FILLING
2 (8-ounce) containers heavy cream
1 (3.4-ounce) package instant vanilla pudding mix

¼ cup milk

TOPPING
¼ cup milk
⅓ cup cocoa
¾ cup sugar

Pinch salt
2 tablespoons butter, melted
1 teaspoon vanilla

Filling: Whip heavy cream on high speed and, as soon as it starts to thicken, add vanilla pudding. Whip a few more seconds and gradually add milk.

Topping: Combine milk, cocoa, sugar and salt to a paste in a saucepan. Boil about 1 minute on low heat, stirring constantly. Remove from heat and add butter and vanilla. Mix well and let cool.

Assembly: Place a layer of graham crackers in a 13 x 9 x 2-inch glass dish. Spread half pudding mixture over crackers. Repeat. Top with a third layer of graham crackers. Cover with cooled chocolate topping. Refrigerate 8-24 hours.

Prepare Ahead of Time

BAKLAVA

Yields: 2 dozen

BAKLAVA
1 (16-ounce) package phyllo dough
3 cups chopped walnuts

1 cup margarine, melted

SYRUP
1½ cups water
1 cup sugar

2-3 tablespoons fresh lemon juice

Preheat oven to 350°.

Baklava: Spread 4-5 sheets of phyllo dough on a 12 x 17-inch baking sheet. Spread generously with walnuts. Repeat layers until all walnuts are used and phyllo dough is the top layer. Using a very sharp knife, cut baklava into diamond shapes. Spread melted margarine evenly over baklava. Bake 20-25 minutes or until golden brown. Watch to make sure it does not burn. Cool before serving.

Syrup: Combine ingredients. Boil, then lower heat and simmer 35 minutes until thickened, but not brown or hard. Pour hot syrup over cooled baklava.

BLACK AND WHITES

Yields: 2 dozen

COOKIES
2 sticks margarine
1⅓ cups sugar
4 eggs

2 teaspoons salt
4 cups flour

WHITE ICING
2 cups confectioners' sugar
½ teaspoon vanilla
4 tablespoons hot water

2 tablespoons oil
Drop of corn syrup

BLACK ICING
1½ cups confectioners' sugar
½ cup cocoa
4 tablespoons hot water

1 tablespoon oil
Drop of corn syrup

Preheat oven to 375°. Cream together margarine and sugar. Add eggs. Add salt and flour. Mix until combined. Form into balls and slightly flatten on an ungreased cookie sheet. Bake about 15 minutes. When cool, smear on icing, covering one half of cookie with white icing and the other with "black". (If icing is too thick, add water. If it is too runny, add more confectioners' sugar.)

Moist and Minty Brownies

Yields: 1 dozen

1¼ cups all-purpose flour
½ teaspoon baking soda
¼ teaspoon salt
¾ cup sugar
½ cup margarine
2 tablespoons water

1 (10-ounce) package semi-sweet
    chocolate chips
1 teaspoon vanilla extract
2 eggs
12 crème de menthe candies

Preheat oven to 350°. In a bowl, combine flour, baking soda and salt; set aside. In a saucepan, combine sugar, margarine and water. Bring to a boil; remove from heat. Add 1 cup chocolate chips and vanilla, stirring until morsels are melted and mixture is smooth. Transfer to large bowl. Add eggs, one at a time, and beat well. Stir in flour mixture and remaining chocolate chips. Spread into a greased 8-inch square baking pan. Bake 25-35 minutes, until center is set. Remove from oven, immediately place candies on top of brownies, allow to melt and spread evenly over top.

Mocha Mousse

Yields: 8 servings

3 ounces unsweetened chocolate
⅓ cup water
¾ cup sugar
3 egg yolks

1 tablespoon instant coffee
1 cup heavy cream
½ teaspoon vanilla

Stir chocolate and water in a heavy saucepan and heat slowly. When chocolate is melted, add sugar and cook over low heat 2 minutes, stirring constantly. Beat egg yolks in a bowl until they are lemon-colored. Add chocolate mixture to the eggs, beating constantly. Blend in instant coffee and cool. Whip the cream, add vanilla and fold into cooled chocolate mixture, saving some whipped cream for topping. Pour into a 1-quart mold. Refrigerate at least 4 hours. Top off with whipped cream.

Very rich and chocolaty!

Prepare Ahead of Time

Desserts

MEXICAN CHOCOLATE TORTE

Yields: 12 servings

CAKE

5 ounces unsweetened baking
    chocolate
½ cup oil
1½ cups sugar
4 eggs

1 teaspoon vanilla
½ cup corn syrup
1 cup flour
Pinch of salt

GLAZE

4 ounces chocolate chips
1 tablespoon oil
1 tablespoon corn syrup

1 teaspoon vanilla
1 tablespoon milk

TOPPING

Chocolate-covered coffee beans

Preheat oven to 350°. Line bottom of 9-inch pie pan with parchment paper.

Cake: Melt chocolate and oil together in glass bowl in microwave. Add sugar and stir until dissolved. Let cool. Add eggs, vanilla and corn syrup, blend. Add flour and salt, stir well. Pour into pie pan, bake 30 minutes. Cool. Loosen sides with knife, turn over onto plate, peel off paper. Flip onto serving plate. Glaze. Decorate with chocolate-covered coffee beans.

Glaze: Melt chocolate chips with oil. Stir in syrup, vanilla and milk. Mix until smooth. Add a little more milk if necessary. Spread thin layer on cooled torte.

APPLE-CREAM CHEESE TORTE
Yields: 8 servings

CRUST
½ cup butter
⅓ cup sugar

¼ teaspoon vanilla
1 cup flour

FILLING
1 (8-ounce) package cream cheese,
    softened
¼ cup sugar
1 egg
½ teaspoon vanilla

⅓ cup sugar
¾ teaspoon cinnamon
6 cups tart apples, sliced and peeled
¼ cup almonds, sliced

Preheat oven to 450°.

Crust: Cream butter, sugar and vanilla. Blend in flour. Pat dough onto bottom and about 1 inch up sides of a 9½ x 2-inch springform pan.

Filling: In a medium bowl, blend together cream cheese and ¼ cup sugar until smooth. Add egg and vanilla. Beat until smooth. Pour into prepared pan. In a large bowl, combine other ⅓ cup sugar and cinnamon. Add apples and toss until well coated. Arrange apples over cheese layer and sprinkle with almonds. Bake 10 minutes. Reduce temperature to 400° and continue baking 35 minutes more or until apples are tender. Cool on wire rack. Refrigerate.

The almonds make this dish especially tasty.

MANDEL BREAD

Yields: 2 dozen slices

STEP 1

1 cup sugar	3 eggs
½ cup oil	1 teaspoon vanilla

STEP 2

3 cups flour	1 cup almonds or other nuts, chopped
2 teaspoons baking powder	6 ounces pareve mini chocolate chips

Preheat oven to 350°. Grease cookie sheets. Mix Step 1 ingredients together. Then mix Step 2 ingredients together. Blend Step 1 and Step 2 mixes together. Turn out on floured board and knead. Divide into 3 parts and make loaves. Bake 30 minutes. Slice loaves, place slices on their sides. Bake an additional 15 minutes.

CHOCOLATE CRINKLE TOP COOKIES

Yields: 2 dozen

2 cups chocolate chips, divided	6 tablespoons soft margarine
1½ cups flour	1½ teaspoons vanilla
1½ teaspoons baking powder	2 eggs
1 cup sugar	½ cup confectioners' sugar

Preheat oven to 350°. Melt 1 cup chocolate chips. Cool slightly. Combine flour and baking powder. Beat sugar, margarine and vanilla until creamy. Add melted chocolate and eggs one at a time. Gradually beat in flour. Stir in remaining 1 cup chocolate chips. Cover and chill. Shape dough into 1½-inch balls. Roll in confectioners' sugar. Bake in ungreased pan 10-15 minutes until sides are set but centers are slightly soft.

CRANBERRY PISTACHIO BISCOTTI

Yields: 2 dozen

¼ cup light olive oil
⅔ cup sugar
1 tablespoon vanilla extract
1 teaspoon almond extract
2 eggs
2 egg whites (additional)

1¾ cups flour
¼ teaspoon salt, if pistachios are
   unsalted
1 teaspoon baking powder
1 cup dried cranberries
1 cup chopped pistachio nuts

Preheat oven to 300°. Line cookie sheets with parchment paper. Mix oil and sugar until blended. Mix in extracts; add eggs and egg whites; beat. Combine flour, salt and baking powder; gradually stir in dry ingredients. Stir in dried cranberries and pistachios. Form 3 logs. Bake 35 minutes until light brown. Cool 10 minutes. Turn oven down to 275°. Cut logs on diagonal into ¾-inch slices. Lay slices on their sides and bake 8-10 minutes until dry. Cool before serving.

CHIPLESS BLONDIES

Yields: 20-24 bars

1¼ cups flour
1¼ teaspoons baking powder
½ teaspoon salt
⅔ cup butter or margarine, room
    temperature
½ cup granulated sugar
⅔ cup brown sugar, packed

1 teaspoon vanilla extract
2 teaspoons grated orange zest
1 teaspoon grated lemon zest
2 eggs
2 teaspoons milk
1 cup almonds, chopped or slivered

Preheat oven to 350°. Lightly grease 9-inch square baking pan. In a bowl, combine flour, baking powder and salt; mix well and set aside. In a food processor or electric mixer, mix butter and granulated sugar until light and fluffy. Add brown sugar; beat again until fluffy. Add vanilla and grated zests; mix well. Add eggs one at a time; beat well. Blend in milk. Stir in flour mixture just to mix. Stir in almonds. Bake in center of oven, about 30 minutes or until toothpick comes out barely moist. Cool in pan on rack. When cool, cover with foil; let stand 8 hours or overnight.

Good plain dessert for those who do not care for chocolate.

STRAWBERRY ROLLUPS

Yields: 2 dozen

DOUGH
2 cups flour
Pinch of salt

½ cup vegetable oil
¼ cup apple juice

FILLING
¼ cup strawberry preserves
**½ cup sugar mixed with ½ teaspoon
cinnamon**

½ cup pecans, chopped, optional

Preheat oven to 375°. Place flour and salt in a medium bowl, mix well. Add oil and juice, and mix very lightly, tossing with fork until all liquid is absorbed (too much mixing will make dough hard). Divide dough in half. Put one half between 2 sheets of wax paper and roll out to ⅛-inch. Remove top sheet. Spread dough with half of preserves, then sprinkle with about half the pecans and one-third of the cinnamon sugar. Use wax paper to help you roll dough (jelly-roll fashion), pulling dough away from paper as you roll. Seal edge by moistening with water. Crimp ends or tuck in as you roll. Place on ungreased jelly-roll pan, seam side down. Repeat for second piece of dough. Sprinkle rollups with cinnamon sugar. Score each roll at 1-inch intervals. Bake 35-40 minutes. Cut into pieces while still warm. Do not over bake. Dough should be light brown and firm to touch.

ICED COFFEE CAKE

Yields: 12 Servings

TOPPING

6 tablespoons butter

1½ cups sugar

1 cup flour

3 teaspoons cinnamon

CAKE

½ pound butter

3 cups flour, sifted

1 teaspoon baking powder

1 teaspoon baking soda

1 cup sugar

3 eggs

1 cup sour cream

1 teaspoon vanilla extract

ICING

½ cup confectioners' sugar

½ teaspoon vanilla extract

3 teaspoons water

Preheat oven to 350°. In a small mixing bowl, cut butter into dry topping ingredients until mixture forms small chunks; set aside. In a large mixing bowl, cream butter for cake. Add dry ingredients in batches, alternating with wet — eggs, sour cream, and vanilla. Beat well until blended. Spread half of batter into greased and floured 13 x 9 x 2-inch pan. Pour half of topping over batter. Pour remaining batter over filling. Sprinkle with remaining topping. Bake 45-50 minutes. Allow to cool. In a small bowl, mix sugar, vanilla and water for thin icing. Drizzle over cooled cake.

CHOCOLATE MOUSSE CHEESECAKE

Yields: 8-10 Servings

CRUST
1 stick butter
18 graham crackers, crushed

¼ cup sugar

CAKE
2 pounds cream cheese, softened
1½ cups sugar
1½ teaspoons lemon juice

Pinch of salt
4 eggs

TOPPING
5 ounces bittersweet chocolate, chopped
1½ cups heavy cream

1 teaspoon vanilla
¼ cup sugar
Chocolate shavings, optional

Preheat oven to 350°.

Crust: Mix all ingredients and press into 9-inch springform pan.

Cake: Beat cream cheese and sugar until soft. Add eggs one at a time. Mix in lemon juice and salt. Pour filling into crust and bake 45 minutes-1 hour or until center jiggles only slightly. Cool completely.

Topping: Melt chocolate in saucepan and cool slightly. Whip cream and vanilla until they form soft peaks. Gradually beat in sugar and continue to beat until cream is stiff. Fold ¼ of whipped cream into chocolate until combined, then add remaining whipped cream. Refrigerate topping until spreadable. Spread evenly on top of cake. Decorate with chocolate shavings.

Peanut Butter Cheesecake

Yields: 8-10 servings

CRUST
1 (12-ounce) box vanilla wafers
½ cup sugar

3 tablespoons butter, melted

FILLING
1 pound cream cheese, room
    temperature
1½ cups sugar
1 (6-ounce) jar creamy peanut butter
5 eggs

½ cup sour cream
2 teaspoons fresh lemon juice
¾-1 cup semi-sweet chocolate chips,
    optional

TOPPING
1 cup sour cream
¾ cup semi-sweet chocolate chips,
    melted

½ cup sugar

Preheat oven to 350°.

Crust: Butter bottom and sides of a 9-inch springform pan. Combine all ingredients in processor and process to uniform crumbs. Press mixture onto bottom and sides of prepared pan.

Filling: Combine all ingredients except chocolate chips in processor and blend until smooth. Add chocolate chips and mix 10 seconds using on/off turns. Spread filling in crust. Bake until center of filling is firm, 70-80 minutes. Let stand at room temperature 15 minutes before adding topping.

Topping: Blend all ingredients. Spread over cheesecake. Bake 10 minutes. Let cake cool, then refrigerate at least 3 hours before serving.

Creamy and delicious.

CHOCOLATE MOUSSE PIE

Yields: 6-8 servings

CRUST
1 package chocolate filled sandwich
    cookies, crushed

¾ stick butter, melted

MOUSSE
18 ounces semi-sweet baking
    chocolate, chopped
4 eggs, separated

2 whole eggs
2½ pints heavy cream
6 teaspoons confectioners' sugar

Preheat oven to 350°.

Crust: Mix ingredients together; pat over bottom and sides of a 10-inch springform pan. Bake 10 minutes.

Mousse: Melt chocolate in double boiler. Whisk in egg yolks, one at a time, until blended. Add whole eggs. Beat egg whites until stiff. Beat 2 pints heavy cream with sugar until stiff. Combine all ingredients in mixer; beat on low speed until mixed. Pour into crust. Whip remaining ½ pint heavy cream with confectioners' sugar until thick. Decorate cake top with whipped cream using pastry bag with rose tip.

Raspberry Chocolate Buttercream Bars

Yields: 36 bars

BASE
4 ounces unsweetened chocolate, cut into pieces
½ cup margarine
2 cups sugar
¼ teaspoon salt
1 teaspoon vanilla
4 eggs
1 cup all-purpose or unbleached flour

FILLING
½ cup seedless raspberry preserves
2 ounces semi-sweet chocolate, cut into pieces
1 ounce unsweetened chocolate, cut into pieces
⅓ cup sugar
¼ cup water
2 eggs
1 cup margarine, cut into small pieces, softened

GLAZE
1 ounce unsweetened chocolate, cut into pieces
1 tablespoon margarine

Preheat oven to 350°.

Base: Grease 13 x 9 x 2-inch pan. In a small saucepan over low heat, melt unsweetened chocolate and margarine, stirring constantly; remove from heat. Cool. In large bowl, beat sugar, salt, vanilla and eggs. Stir in melted chocolate mixture just until blended. Stir in flour just until blended. Spread mixture evenly in prepared pan. Bake 25-30 minutes or until set. Cool.

Filling: Spread raspberry preserves over base. In a small saucepan over low heat, melt semi-sweet chocolate and unsweetened chocolate, stirring constantly. Remove from heat. In another small saucepan, bring sugar and water to a boil. Boil 1 minute. In a large bowl, beat eggs until frothy. Gradually add sugar-water mixture to eggs and beat on highest speed 5 minutes or until thick and lemon colored. Gradually add margarine a small piece at a time, beating well after each addition. Add melted chocolate and beat until smooth. Spread filling carefully over preserves.

Glaze: In small saucepan over low heat, melt unsweetened chocolate and margarine, stirring constantly. Drizzle over filling. Refrigerate 1 hour. Cut into bars. Store in refrigerator.

Lemon-Ginger Bars

Yields: 16 bars

CRUST
1 cup all-purpose flour
¼ cup confectioners' sugar
1 tablespoon lemon zest
½ teaspoon fresh grated ginger
Pinch of salt
½ cup chilled, unsalted butter

FILLING
2 tablespoons all-purpose flour
1½ cups confectioners' sugar
½ teaspoon baking powder
Pinch of salt
3 large eggs at room temperature
6 teaspoons fresh lemon juice

TOPPING
1 pinch ground ginger
1 teaspoon confectioners' sugar

Preheat oven to 350°. Butter an 8-inch square baking pan.

Crust: Whisk together flour, confectioners' sugar, lemon zest, ginger and salt. Cut in the butter until mixture resembles crumbs. Knead dough until it just holds together. Dust your hands with flour, transfer dough to the baking pan, and press it evenly over the bottom. Bake about 20 minutes, until just lightly golden brown. Remove and allow to cool.

Filling: Whisk together flour, confectioners' sugar, baking powder, and salt until well mixed. In another bowl, beat eggs with electric mixer at high speed 3-5 minutes, until they triple in volume and are light and fluffy. Reduce mixer speed, add dry mixture, and continue to mix until blended. Add lemon juice and mix again until blended. Pour filling over crust.

Bake 18-20 minutes, until filling is set in center and doesn't shake. Remove and set aside to cool. Just before serving, mix together ground ginger and teaspoon of confectioners' sugar and sift over the top. Cut into 2-inch squares.

The ginger also can be left out, if you prefer.

FUDGE CUPS

Yields: 48 servings

CUPS

1 cup sugar
½ cup margarine, softened
1 egg
2 ounces unsweetened chocolate,
    melted, cooled

¼ teaspoon salt
½ teaspoon vanilla
1¾ cups all-purpose or
    unbleached flour

FILLING

1½ cups sugar
1½ ounces unsweetened chocolate,
    cut into pieces
⅓ cup soy milk

¼ cup margarine
3 tablespoons corn syrup
⅛ teaspoon salt
1 teaspoon vanilla

Preheat oven to 350°.

Cups: Grease miniature muffin cups or line with paper baking cups. In a large bowl, cream sugar and margarine until light and fluffy. Blend in egg, beat well. Stir in chocolate, salt and vanilla, mix well. Blend in flour; mix well. Shape dough into 1-inch balls. Press ball in bottom and up sides of prepared muffin cups. Bake 8-10 minutes. Cool 5-10 minutes; remove from pan with small spatula.

Filling: In a small saucepan over low heat, cook sugar, unsweetened chocolate, soy milk, margarine, corn syrup and salt until chocolate is melted, stirring occasionally. Bring mixture to a boil; boil 1 minute. Remove from heat, stir in vanilla. Beat to cool slightly; spoon into cups.

Any leftover dough from the cups makes terrific cookies. Just roll into small balls, dust with sugar, flatten, and bake on a greased cookie sheet at 350°, 12 minutes or until they rise slightly and begin to crack.

RUGELACH

Yields: 48 servings

1 pound cream cheese, softened
1 pound unsalted butter, softened
2 cups flour
½ cup plus 2 tablespoons sugar
1 tablespoon ground cinnamon

½ cup apricot, raspberry, or strawberry preserves
1 cup finely chopped pecans
1 cup raisins

Mix cream cheese, butter, and flour in a large bowl by hand until creamy and well incorporated. (Dough will be very soft and sticky.) Divide dough into 4 portions; shape into balls and place each on a sheet of plastic wrap. Wrap plastic wrap around each ball to enclose. Freeze until hard (about 2-3 hours).

Preheat oven to 325°. Set out each ball of dough as needed to soften slightly. Cover baking sheets with foil or parchment paper. Mix sugar and cinnamon; set aside. Roll out a ball of dough into a thin disk (just less than ⅛ inch thickness) on a lightly floured surface. Spread dough evenly with 1-2 tablespoons preserves, followed by pecans, cinnamon sugar and raisins, making sure there is enough of each ingredient left over for the other portions of dough. Reserve part of cinnamon sugar for topping.

Cut the disk into triangles (see diagram). Roll up each wedge, starting from wide end, inward like a snail. Place, away from each other and with point sides down, on prepared baking sheets. Sprinkle with cinnamon sugar on top. You may place cookie sheet with unbaked rugelach in refrigerator while you make the rest of the rugelach.

Bake 25 minutes or until lightly browned. Immediately transfer to wire rack to cool.

For this recipe to be a success, freeze the dough very well and work as fast as you can when rolling it and making the rugelach. They come out very light and fluffy. Some butter will come out during the baking process.

Worth the Effort

SELECT BIBLIOGRAPHY

Much Depends on Dinner, Margaret Visser, Grove Press, 1987.

The Book of Jewish Food, Claudia Roden, Alfred A. Knopf, Inc. 1996.

The Food Chronology, James Trager, Henry Holt & Co., 1995.

The Jewish Holiday Cookbook, Gloria Kaufer Greene, Times Books, 1985.

The Jewish Holiday Kitchen, Joan Nathan, Schocken, 1979.

The International Kosher Cookbook, edited by Batia Plotch & Patricia Cobe, Fawcett Books, 1992.

The World of Jewish Cooking, Gil Marks, Simon & Schuster, 1996.

RECIPE INDEX

INDEX

F

G

GROUND BEEF, SEE MEAT

H

I

ICE CREAM, *SEE DESSERTS*

J

K

L

LAMB, *SEE MEAT*

M

MEAT
BEEF
Brisket

Chuck

Ground

Ribs

Salami

Steak

Stew Meat

BISON

LAMB

S

Salad Dressings

Salads

Salmon, See Fish

Side Dishes & Vegetables

MEASURING DEVICES

Tip: **Keep two basic measuring sets for the kitchen;** one for liquid and one for dry ingredients.

Tip: Never use tableware for measuring

- Set of measuring spoons – **¼ tsp, ½ tsp, 1 tsp, 1 Tbsp**
- Set of measuring cups – **¼ cup, ⅓ cup, ½ cup, 1 cup**
- Measuring pitcher (glass or plastic, see-through with graduated markings) better for liquids – **1 cup/½ pt, 2 cup/1 pt, 4 cup/1 qt**
- Scales – 2 - 4 pound capacity. Balance type scales tend to be more accurate than spring scales.

COMMON MEASUREMENTS AND EQUIVALENTS

3 teaspoons. . . . . . . = ... 1 tablespoon

1 tablespoon . . . . . . = ...3 teaspoons or ½ fluid ounce

2 tablespoons. . . . . . = ... ⅛ cup or 1 fluid ounce

3 tablespoons. . . . . . = ...1½ fluid ounces or 1 jigger

4 tablespoons. . . . . . = ... ¼ cup or 2 fluid ounces

8 tablespoons. . . . . . = ... ½ cup or 4 fluid ounces

12 tablespoons . . . . . = ... ¾ cup or 6 fluid ounces

16 tablespoons . . . . . = ...1 cup or 8 fluid ounces or ½ pint

2 cups . . . . = ... 1 pint or 16 fluid ounces

1 quart . . . . = ... 2 pints or 4 cups or 32 fluid ounces

1 gallon. . . . . = ... 4 quarts or 8 pints or 16 cups or 128 fluid ounces

DRY MEASURING TIPS

- **Do not pour dry ingredients into measuring device while it is over mixing bowl;** this eliminates accidental spilling or overflow of the ingredient.

- **Measure dry ingredients over a plate or paper** to be able to put overflows back into original container.

- Scoop or fill the exact-size measuring device (cup or teaspoon) and then tap gently once or twice with knife (eliminates air pockets) **and level with knife** to the top surface of the device. Try to avoid using larger devices.

- When measuring by weight, **zero out the container on the scales first.**

- Make sure you **measure the final form** called for in the recipe (chopped, diced, sliced, etc) See "sifted" below.

- **Flour, *sifted* means measure first,** then sift. *Sifted flour* **means sift first, then measure.** The location of the word "sifted" defines the procedure.

- If not using a measure, as with dry spices or salt and pepper, **first shake the amount into your hand** and then into the mixing bowl or pot. This prevents over-seasoning which may be difficult to undo once added.

- **A pinch** means ⅛ **tsp or less** of a dry ingredient. A **dash,** usually referring to a liquid (but not always), means a 1 or 2 drops or ⅛ tsp for dry.

- Sticky ingredients such as brown sugar or raisins should be **packed tightly** in the device for accuracy.

DRY MEASURE CONVERSION

1 cup	8 fl oz	16 Tbs	48 tsp	237 ml
¾ cup	6 fl oz	12 Tbs	36 tsp	177 ml
⅔ cup	5⅓ fl oz	10⅔ Tbs	32 tsp	158 ml
½ cup	4 fl oz	8 Tbs	24 tsp	118 ml
⅓ cup	2⅔ fl oz	5⅓ Tbs	16 tsp	79 ml
¼ cup	2 fl oz	4 Tbs	12 tsp	59 ml
⅛ cup	1 fl oz	2 Tbs	6 tsp	30 ml
¹⁄₁₆ cup	½ fl oz	1 Tbs	3 tsp	15 ml
¼ cup	⅛ fl oz	½ Tbs	1 tsp	5 ml

Liquid Measuring Tips

- **Do not pour liquids into measuring device while it is over mixing bowl.**

- **Use a clear measuring device with graduated scale** placed on level surface. Bend down to sight along the marking for accuracy. Don't raise the cup to eye level…it won't be level.

- **Exact-sized devices,** such as teaspoons and ½ cups, must be filled to the rim or marking indicated.

- When measuring sticky liquids, such as honey or syrup, **first coat the device with a tiny amount of vegetable oil or spray.** The syrup will release more easily from the device.

- Fats such as **butter, margarine and/or shortening, pack better and measure more accurately at room temperature.**

Liquid Measure Conversion

1 gal	4 qt	8 pt	16 cups	128 fl oz	3.79L		
½ gal	2 qt	4 pt	8 cups	64 fl oz	1.89L		
¼ gal	1 qt	2 pt	4 cups	32 fl oz	.95L		
	½ qt	1 pt	2 cups	16 fl oz	.47L		
	¼ qt	½ pt	1 cup	8 fl oz	.24L		
			½ cup	4 fl oz	.12L	8 Tbs	24 tsp
			¼ cup	2 fl oz	.06L	4 Tbs	12 tsp
			⅛ cup	1 fl oz	.03L	2 Tbs	6 tsp
				½ fl oz	.015L	1 Tbs	3 tsp

Metric Conversions

WEIGHT EQUIVALENTS

These are not exact weight equivalents, but have been rounded up or down slightly to make measuring easier.

AMERICAN	METRIC
¼ ounce	.7 grams
½ ounce	.15 grams
1 ounce	.30 grams
8 ounces (½ pound)	.225 grams
16 ounces (1 pound)	.450 grams
2¼ pounds	.1 kilogram

VOLUME EQUIVALENTS

These are not exact volume equivalents, but have been rounded up or down slightly to make measuring easier.

AMERICAN	METRIC
¼ teaspoon	1.25 milliliters
½ teaspoon	2.5 milliliters
1 teaspoon	.5 milliliters
½ tablespoon (1½ teaspoons)	7.5 milliliters
1 tablespoon (3 teaspoons)	.15 milliliters
¼ cup (4 tablespoons)	.60 milliliters
⅓ cup (5 tablespoons)	.75 milliliters
½ cup (8 tablespoons)	.125 milliliters
⅔ cup (10 tablespoons)	.150 milliliters
¾ cup (12 tablespoons)	.175 milliliters
1 cup (16 tablespoons)	.250 milliliters
1¼ cups	.300 milliliters
1½ cups	.350 milliliters
1 pint (2 cups)	.500 milliliters
2½ cups	.625 milliliters
1 quart (4 cups)	1 litre

OVEN TEMPERATURE EQUIVALENTS

OVEN	FAHRENHEIT	CELSIUS
very cool	250-275	130-140
cool	300	150
warm	325	170
moderate	350	180
moderately hot	375	190
moderately hot	400	200
hot	425	220
very hot	450	230
very hot	475	250

DINNER PLANNER

Below is listed the uncooked ingredient amount to purchase in order to yield an average per-guest cooked serving portion of about 6 oz

INGREDIENT	TO BUY
Beef (boneless, steaks/roasts/stews)	7-8 oz
Beef (bone-in, steaks/roasts)	8-10 oz
Beef (short ribs)	14-16 oz
Veal (cutlets)	4-5 oz
Veal (bone-in, chops)	5-6 oz
Chicken (boneless, breasts/thighs)	6-7 oz
Chicken (bone-in, parts)	7-8 oz
Chicken (whole, broiler/fryer)	8-9 oz

COOKWARE CAPACITIES

It is not always possible to have available the exact size pan called for in given recipe. All sizes below are rounded to the nearest ½ inch cup. These conversions may be helpful as a guide in modifying a recipe to fit a particular pan. Plan on about ¼ cup error rate depending on actual pan size. Baking times may also change with pan configuration.

DESCRIPTION	CUPS TO FILL
Round baking pans	
7" x 2½" (springform)	7
8" x 1½" (cake)	4
8" x 2½" (springform)	8
9" x 1½" (cake)	6
9" x 2½" (springform)	9
9½" x 2½" (springform)	11
10" x 2" (cake)	10
Regular baking pans	
8" x 8" x 1½"	6
8" x 8" x 2"	7
9" x 9" x 1½"	8
9" x 13" x 2"	16
Pie pans	
8"	4
9"	7
Bread loaf pans	
6" x 3" x 2"	2
7½" x 3¾" x 2¼"	4
8½" x 4½" x 2½"	5½
9" x 5" x 3"	8
Muffin pans	
12 large	3½
12 mini	1½

EMERGENCY SUBSTITUTIONS OF INGREDIENTS

At one time or another, most cooks find themselves without an ingredient needed to complete a recipe. The following substitutions can be made with satisfactory results in most recipes. The exception would be baked goods for which – if at all possible – it is safer not to use substitutions.

IF THE RECIPE CALLS FOR:		SUBSTITUTE:
ARROWROOT — 1 tablespoon	=	1½ tablespoons all-purpose flour OR 2¼ teaspoons cornstarch, potato starch or rice starch
BAKING POWDER, double acting	=	¼ teaspoon baking soda plus ⅝ teaspoon cream of tartar OR ¼ teaspoon baking soda plus ½ cup buttermilk or sour milk (reduce liquid in recipe by ½ cup) OR ¼ teaspoon baking soda plus ⅜ cup molasses (reduce liquid in recipe by ¼ cup; adjust sweetener) OR 1½ teaspoons phosphate or tartrate baking powder
BREAD CRUMBS, dry – 1 cup	=	¾ cup cracker crumbs
BUTTERMILK or SOUR MILK – 1 cup	=	1 cup plain yogurt OR 1 tablespoon vinegar or lemon juice plus enough milk to equal 1 cup (let stand 5 minutes) OR 1¾ teaspoons cream of tartar plus 1 cup milk
CAJUN SPICE, 1 tablespoon	=	½ teaspoon each white pepper, garlic powder, onion powder, ground red pepper, paprika and black pepper
CHOCOLATE, semi-sweet – 6 ounces chips	=	½ ounce unsweetened chocolate plus 1 tablespoon granulated sugar
CHOCOLATE, unsweetened – 1 ounce	=	3 tablespoons unsweetened cocoa plus 1 tablespoon butter or margarine OR 3 tablespoons carob powder plus 2 tablespoons water

IF THE RECIPE CALLS FOR:		SUBSTITUTE:
CORNSTARCH – 1 tablespoon	=	2 tablespoons all-purpose flour OR 2 teaspoons arrowroot
CORN SYRUP, dark – 1 cup	=	¾ light corn syrup plus ¼ cup light molasses
CORN SYRUP, light or dark – 1 cup	=	1¼ cups granulated or packed brown sugar plus ¼ cup liquid (Use whatever liquid recipe calls for.)
CRACKER CRUMBS – 1 cup	=	1¼ cups bread crumbs
CREAM, half-and-half, – 1 cup	=	1½ tablespoons butter plus enough whole milk to equal 1 cup OR ½ cup light cream plus ½ cup whole milk
CREAM, light (20% fat) – 1 cup	=	3 tablespoons butter plus enough milk to equal 1 cup
CREAM, sour – 1 cup	=	1 cup plain yogurt OR ¾ cup sour milk, buttermilk or plain yogurt plus ⅓ cup butter OR 1 tablespoon lemon juice plus enough evaporated whole milk to equal 1 cup
CREAM, whipping (36-40% fat)	=	¾ cup whole milk plus ⅓ cup butter
EGG, whole – 1 egg	=	2 egg yolks plus 1 tablespoon cold water OR 3½ tablespoons thawed frozen egg or egg substitute OR 2½ tablespoons powdered whole egg plus an equal amount of water
EGG, white – 1 white	=	2 tablespoons thawed frozen egg white OR 1 tablespoon powdered egg white plus 2 tablespoons water
EGG, yolk – 2 yolks	=	1 whole egg (for thickening sauces, etc.)
1 LARGE YOLK	=	3½ teaspoons thawed frozen yolk OR 2 tablespoons powdered yolk plus 2 teaspoons water (for baking)
FLOUR (for thickening) –	=	1 tablespoon cornstarch, potato starch or rice starch OR 4 teaspoons arrowroot OR 2 tablespoons quick-cooking tapioca

IF THE RECIPE CALLS FOR:		SUBSTITUTE:
FLOUR – 1 cup sifted all-purpose	=	1 cup minus 2 tablespoons unsifted all-purpose flour
FLOUR – 1 cup sifted cake	=	1 cup minus 2 tablespoons sifted all-purpose flour
FLOUR – 1 cup sifted self-rising	=	1 cup sifted all-purpose flour plus 1½ teaspoons baking powder and ⅛ teaspoon salt
GARLIC – 1 small clove	=	⅛ teaspoon garlic powder
HERB – snipped fresh, 1 tablespoon	=	½ - 1 teaspoon dry herb, crushed
HONEY – 1 cup	=	1¼ cups granulated sugar plus ¼ cup liquid (Use whatever liquid recipe calls for.)
LEMON JUICE – 1 teaspoon	=	½ teaspoon vinegar
MILK, nonfat (skim) – 1 cup	=	⅓ cup nonfat powdered milk plus ¾ cup water
MILK, sour – 1 cup	=	1 tablespoon lemon juice or white vinegar plus enough milk to equal 1 cup (let stand 5 minutes)
MILK, whole – 1 cup	=	1 cup nonfat (skim) milk plus 2 tablespoons butter or margarine
MUSTARD, prepared – 1 tablespoon	=	1 teaspoon powdered mustard
ONION, chopped, 1 small (⅓ cup)	=	1 teaspoon onion powder or 1 tablespoon dried, minced onion
TOMATO JUICE – 1 cup	=	½ cup tomato sauce plus ½ cup water
TOMATO SAUCE – 1 cup	=	⅜ cup tomato paste plus ½ cup water
VINEGAR – 1 teaspoon	=	2 teaspoons lemon juice
YOGURT – 1 cup	=	1 cup buttermilk OR 1 cup milk plus 1 tablespoon lemon juice

FOOD STORAGE

DRY STORAGE

The three constants for retaining the freshness of already dry ingredients and some vegetables are **dry, dark, and cool.** Humidity, light and heat all promote the growth of organisms that will spoil the food. Many root vegetables such as onions, potatoes, turnips and beets may be kept indoors in dark, dry, airy bins for a month or more. Always take all vegetables out of bags for storing. Dried pastas, peas, beans and grains, as well as herbs and spices, should be kept in sealed containers away from heat and light. Select a cupboard away from appliances or a humidity controlled basement.

ITEM	REFRIGERATOR	FREEZER
Apples	1 mo	N/R
Berries	3 da	10 mo[1]
Butter (see margarine below)	2 wk	2 mo
Cheese, soft (cream, cottage, Brie, feta)	1 wk	N/R
Cheese, hard (Parmesan, whole)	4 wk	6 mo
Condiments (ketchup, mustard)	12 mo	N/R
Eggs, in shell	3 wk	N/R
Egg yolks or whites separated	3 da	12 mo
Eggs, hard boiled	1 wk	N/R
Egg substitute, unopened	1 wk	12 mo
Fish, fresh	1 da	8 mo
Fish, uncooked previously frozen	1 da	N/R
Melons	5 da	N/R
Meats, roasts	5 da	12 mo
Meats, ground (beef, chicken)	2 da	4 mo
Meats, steaks, chops	5 da	12 mo
Meats, cooked	4 da	3 mo
Meats, luncheon, hot dogs, unopened	2 wk	2 mo
Meats, luncheon opened (resealed)	1 wk	2 mo
Onions, cut pieces (wrapped)	3 da	N/R
Peaches, pears, pineapple	4 da	N/R
Poultry, raw, whole	2 da	12 mo
Poultry, raw, parts	2 da	9 mo
Poultry, cooked, parts and pieces	4 da	4 mo
Vegetables, carrots, celery, radishes	2 wk	8 mo[2]

Vegetables, potatoes . . . . .N/R . . . . .N/R

Vegetables, peas, beans, broccoli . . . . 5 days . . . . 8 mo

Vegetables, cooked, leftovers . . . . 2 days . . . . 8 mo

Vegetables, greens . . . . 5 days . . . . .N/R

N/R=not recommended

¹ To prepare berries, trim as desired, rinse, and dry gently with paper towels. Package or quick freeze.

² To prepare vegetables, trim as desired, rinse. Plunge them into large pot of rapidly boiling water (on high heat). Boil 2 to 4 minutes, depending on thickness of vegetable. Using strainer, move vegetables to large pot of prepared ice water and stir to cool. This is blanching. Strain vegetables again and use paper towels to dry. Package or quick freeze.

QUICK FREEZING

Very lightly spray a jelly-roll pan with cooking spray. Place prepared berries or vegetables on pan so they do not touch each other. Do not cover. Freeze until firm, 1-2 hours for berries, 2-3 hours for vegetables. Redistribute items into individual freezer bags and return to freezer.

Manna *from* Heaven

Down to Earth Kosher Recipes

Rudlin Torah Academy
12285 Patterson Avenue
Richmond, VA 23238
804-784-9050
www.rudlin.com

Please send me _____ cookbook(s)   @ $26.95 each _____

Shipping and handling $5.00 for first book   @ $ 5.00 each _____

                    $4.00 each additional book   @ $ 4.00 each _____

                                                    SUBTOTAL _____

Virginia residents add 5% sales tax   TAX _____

                                                    TOTAL _____

PLEASE SEND MY COOKBOOKS TO:

Name _____

Address _____

City _____ State _____ Zip_____

Phone _____

E-mail _____

METHOD OF PAYMENT:

◯ CHECK payable to Rudlin Torah Academy

Please charge $ _____ to my
    VISA   MASTERCARD   DISCOVER

Card Number_____ Exp. Date _____

Billing Address _____

Signature _____